CASE STUDIES IN

CULTURAL ANTHROPOLOGY

GENERAL EDITORS
George and Louise Spindler
STANFORD UNIVERSITY

BURGBACH

*Urbanization and Identity
in a German Village*

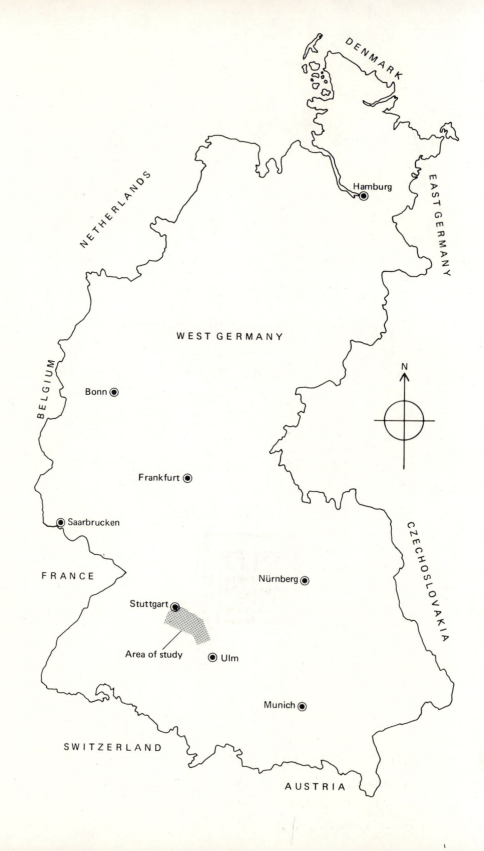

DENMARK

Hamburg

NETHERLANDS

EAST GERMANY

BELGIUM

WEST GERMANY

N

Bonn

Frankfurt

Saarbrucken

FRANCE

CZECHOSLOVAKIA

Nürnberg

Stuttgart

Area of study

Ulm

Munich

SWITZERLAND

AUSTRIA

BURGBACH:
Urbanization and Identity
in a German Village

By

GEORGE D. SPINDLER
and
STUDENT COLLABORATORS
Stanford University

HOLT, RINEHART AND WINSTON, INC.

NEW YORK   CHICAGO   SAN FRANCISCO   ATLANTA
DALLAS   MONTREAL   TORONTO   LONDON   SYDNEY

*This book is dedicated to the hospitable
and helpful people of the Remstal, to the
inspiring students of Stanford University,
and to my wife, Louise, whose help and
counsel were invaluable.*

Cover photos: (1) Weingartner hoeing (courtesy Rick Hanson) and (2) new construction in Burgbach (courtesy Don Camp)

Library of Congress Catalog Card Number: 72–88159
ISBN: 0–03–091883–9
Printed in the United States of America
3 4 5 6   059   9 8 7 6 5 4 3 2 1

Foreword

About the Series

These case studies in cultural anthropology are designed to bring to students, in beginning and intermediate courses in the social sciences, insights into the richness and complexity of human life as it is lived in different ways and in different places. They are written by men and women who have lived in the societies they write about and who are professionally trained as observers and interpreters of human behavior. The authors are also teachers, and in writing their books they have kept the students who will read them foremost in their minds. It is our belief that when an understanding of ways of life very different from one's own is gained, abstractions and generalizations about social structure, cultural values, subsistence techniques, and the other universal categories of human social behavior become meaningful.

About the Author

George Spindler is Professor of Anthropology and Education at Stanford University. He is a Fellow in the American Anthropological Association and was Editor of the *American Anthropologist* from 1962 through 1966. He is the coauthor, with Louise Spindler, of *Dreamers without Power: The Menomini Indians*, also published in this series, and other articles and books about the Menomini and Blood Indians, with whom the Spindlers have intermittently done fieldwork for many years. George Spindler's major interests have been in the psychology of culture change and cultural transmission. A contributor to the anthropology of education, he has edited and authored several books and articles in this field, including, most recently, *Education and Cultural Process*. Related to his interests in acculturation and culture change is his concern with the process of urbanization, an outgrowth of which was his involvement with research in Germany. This work began in 1959, when he and his wife and daughter were with Stanford in Germany Group III at the Study Center near Stuttgart. His actual interest in German culture, however, began during World War II, and it was a field that he was encouraged to pursue in graduate work at the University of Wisconsin immediately after the war. The result of his study was a comparison of German and American responses to constant features of military organization.

About the Book

Writing a case study about a community of 5,000 persons undergoing transformative change in a complex, modern society is a bold undertaking. For anyone to do it on the basis of one's own field work, and *only* one's own, would be very difficult. This case study is possible because the author has drawn from the work of several hundred undergraduate students who have been in residence at Stanford in Germany at various times, and who were studying anthropology. Their main assignment was to do a field study. Though there are certain dangers inherent in using data collected by so many other workers, particularly because most were untrained in anthropology, except for their studies at Stanford in Germany, these dangers are outweighed by the scope and variety of the sample of personnel, behaviors, and groups that could be utilized. The studies also took place over a decade, and some studies were repeated several times. These conditions, too, argue for a certain reliability.

We have tried to keep the scope of the case study narrow enough to make it possible to deal with certain phenomena in some depth. The theme is continuity and change, two processes relevant to most communities in these times.

The intellectual orientation of this case study is drawn from both cultural anthropology and sociology. Explicit development of theoretical models is confined to two crucial points: the concept of social aggregates in Chapter 2 and the instrumental model of cultural systems in Chapter 6. Some relatively novel analyses of forces for cultural persistence are attempted in Chapter 4. The many issues and qualifications that one could become involved with are largely left dormant. Colleagues will find various propositions and applications arguable, and we feel that such arguments should be part of the proper use of this case study. It may be helpful to keep in mind the fact that the author found the conceptual armamentarium of anthropology to be insufficient for the analytic and interpretive engagements he found himself confronting in the study of cultural continuity and urbanization in a complex society.

It is important to remember that this case study is written for students to read so that they will come to a better understanding both of why and how the world is changing, and why it does not change all at once. Of course, the study of any one community can shed light on only some processes, not all. The site of the Burgbach study is not typical of anything, nor is it atypical. It has more in common with all small, changing human communities than it has of difference.

George and Louise Spindler
General Editors

Stanford in Germany
1972

Acknowledgments

Probably no book has ever been written that stood in debt to so many. Without the students of Stanford in Germany Groups III, IV, XVIII, XX, XXIV, and XXVI there would not have been a book. Without the hospitality, patience, and willing cooperation of the many people of the Remstal who helped us to gain an understanding of their way of life, there would not have been a book. Without my wife's encouragement, endurance, and general insight, to say nothing of her help in our fieldwork, there would not have been a book. Without Beth Borgelt, who typed two versions of the manuscript, the first directly from the tape I had used for its dictation while I was in Germany, there never would have been a book. Without the help of Erika Lueders-Salmon, herself a native of a Remstal community (Bad Cannstatt) and a doctoral student at Stanford in the sociology of education, there would not have been a book. Without the precedent set by Richard Warren's study in Rebhausen and Ethel Warren's help with the art work for the Instrumental Activities Inventory, the research and analysis that led to this book would have taken a less adequate form. And without the careful readings and very useful suggestions by colleagues Robert Anderson, Joel Halpern, and Hans Weiler, this book would be less than it is. Thanks everyone!

G. D. S.

Contents

BURGBACH

*Urbanization and Identity
in a German Village*

The Remstal in the vicinity of Burgbach. The villages, clearly separate in this picture, are growing together as urbanization takes place. Flatland agricultural plots in different crops and various stages of fallow, vineyards on terraced slopes, fruit gardens, and the forest, predominantly black fir, are all clearly visible. (Printed with the acknowledgement: Freigegeben vom Reg. Präsidium Nord-württemberg Nr. 2132081 Luftbild Albrecht Brugger, Stuttgart.)

Introduction

This is a study of the confrontation of the past and the future in a village in southern Germany, one of the many in Europe and elsewhere in the world where dramatic urbanization and industrialization are taking place and a traditional folk community is being overwhelmed by modernization. It is a study of cultural persistence and transformation, of striving for identity where established identities are threatened, of the mutual adaptation of migrant newcomers and natives, of ritualized ways of doing things giving way to technological rationalization, and of the effect of the school and its culture upon children who must adapt to an environment foreign to their teachers and parents.

This case study is the result of an educational experiment. It is based upon the work of Stanford undergraduate students at the Stanford University Center in West Germany as well as that of the author. Their names are listed at the end of the book.

Our purpose while studying together in Germany was not to write a book, but rather to learn something about anthropology and about the Rems Valley and its inhabitants. This is the valley that stretches below the "Burg," the local name given to the Stanford Study Center. The *Remstal* is of considerable historical significance in southern Germany and today is both economically and politically important as a part of Baden-Württemberg.[1]

Our studies of people and events in this valley were not done at a distance. Each student whose work in some way is represented in this case study was directly engaged with his or her instructors, who were the people themselves. The inhabitants of the Remstal were most helpful from the beginning. They recognized that students could not learn about them and their land unless they themselves instructed them. Few doors were closed. Individuals, families, informal and formal groups and associations, the mayors' offices, police departments, county offices, all provided information and instruction. Partly this is because the researchers were young people, eager to learn, who were not passing judgment on what they learned as they learned it. Partly it is because the people of the Remstal are proud of their communities and their social, economic, cultural, and political viability.

The role of the anthropologist-professor was to integrate information that was

---

[1] Baden-Württemberg is a *Land*, a political subunit roughly similar to a province in Canada or a state in the United States.

collected by students, to encourage interpretation by the students themselves, and to interpret further himself, and to guide continued study in relevant and appropriate directions. His primary responsibility within the purpose of the Stanford Study Center was to teach. This teaching was done in two dimensions: to communicate an understanding of the discipline of anthropology and its theory and method; and to teach the particulars, as our understanding grew, of culture, community, and change in the Remstal. The two purposes were joined in the classroom. The content of the latter furnished illustration of the former.

Teaching in this situation required not only the usual transmission of information and generalizations through reading, lecture, and discussion but also the sensitization of students to the problems of transcultural perception and interpretation. This training entered into various phases of the instructional process in the classes and seminars conducted by the author at the Studies Center, but particularly in one phase of instruction that each year took place in the first week of the quarter (Spindler 1973). The major focus was on developing an understanding of general principles governing perception of objects, events, situations, and behaviors in a cultural setting foreign to the observer, and the interpretation of their significance. It became clear both to students and teacher that the probabilities of error in transcultural perception and interpretation are considerable. We know that we have not avoided all such errors in this case study. The sensitization training procedure was a useful step in the direction of curbing the culturally patterned tendencies that produce these errors.

As our understanding of the dynamics of culture and community in the Remstal expanded corresponding to the increasing range and depth of our studies, our focus became continuity and change. It was apparent that the Remstal was an area characterized by considerable cultural conservatism, even though it was, at the same time, urbanizing. A traditional "core" culture centering upon the small villages and their relationship to the land was identified in the early stages of study. During the later phases the processes of urbanization and industrialization dominated, both in the field which we were observing and in our thinking.

The themes of continuity and change will be represented in various ways in the chapters to follow. The analysis centers on a community called "Burgbach" that has certain distinctive characteristics but that nevertheless is representative of an intermediate level of urbanization where links with the past are still apparent. Reference will also be made to a village called Schönhausen. This village is near Burgbach and shares the traditional core culture and exhibits many common features in the adaptation to urbanization but is somewhat different in the pace of its adaptation.

Louise Spindler and I spent some months in Schönhausen as I conducted a study of the elementary school and its influence upon the adaptation of the children who attended it. This study is reported in detail in another publication (Spindler 1973) and is represented in this book in the chapter on schooling.

For over a decade both of the Spindlers have also had extensive personal contacts within Burgbach. We have participated in many discussions with village officials and others about the past, present, and future of Burgbach. We have visited many homes and attended many public events.

The students from Stanford in Germany, Groups III, IV, XX, XXII, XXIV, and XXVI, however, have done all the hard work of data collection.[2] They have spent many hours in the town offices going over files generously made available to them. They have observed in schools, from kindergarten to secondary school. They have interviewed factory managers, housewives, doctors, shop owners, workers, priests, and ministers. They have participated and observed in churches, eating and drinking places, sport clubs, music clubs, youth groups, festivals, and grape harvests. They have worked in factories and in vineyards. And they have all been helped to an understanding of life in the Remstal by their adopted families, who opened their homes to the students as though they were their own children. The range and intensity of their contacts were much greater than would have been possible for a single professional field worker, or even a team of workers. This case study is indeed a result of their work, and of their insights. The people of the Remstal, and particularly of Burgbach, are their collaborators. I hope that my interpretations are worthy of these good works and high interest on the part of both students and Remstäler.

The time period for our observations extends from the fall of 1959 intermittently over twelve years. During this time the Remstal has been continuously changing. No matter what particular point in time we might describe Burgbach, what we describe will not exist as we describe it when anyone reads this case study. This is true for all community studies. The processes of change are more dramatic in Burgbach than in many that anthropologists describe. We have placed our emphasis upon processes that will continue into the future and that have continued for some time. Demographic and other similar data, however, are very time-linked. We have, therefore, centered such data on the period 1969–1970, unless otherwise indicated.

Certain details have been omitted or obscured to protect individuals. We have also used a pseudonym, "Burgbach," even though this is a thin disguise, to protect our community from casual exploitation by the curious, and also to symbolize the fact that the community described is a Remstal community, representative of processes occurring in much the same way, though with individual variations, in the other Remstal communities. "Burgbach" therefore stands for a particular urbanizing village, but also as prototypical for a wider range of phenomena and a wider geographic and cultural area.

IN PROSPECT

This is a case study of an urbanizing, recently folk and land-oriented community. There is much that must be left out, given the reasonable space limitations

[2] This case study was finished in manuscript by August 1971. Minor revisions were made during the spring quarter, 1972, at Stanford in Germany, while the work of Group XXVIII was in progress. Our common concerns are represented in some of the revision and I have benefited from student criticisms of material presented in lectures, but no papers had as yet been completed. I wish to express my thanks, however, for their continuing interest and suggestions.

of the case study format. We cover[3] in Chapter 1, under the title *Time and Land*, the historical foundations for a special identity for Burgbach, and in a preliminary way, consider the relationship of the community to the land around it. In Chapter 2, *What Kinds of People Are There?*, we describe the diversity of present-day Burgbach, as contrasted to the relative homogeneity of the prewar community. We show how the newcomers from outside the Remstal that flooded into Western Germany during the great post-World War II resettlement created a new kind of social structure, one that we think is characteristic of urbanizing communities, where individuals expressing new as well as established life styles form loose aggregates rather than bounded social classes. In Chapter 3, *The Families*, we assemble inside views of seven families, representing distinctive life styles ranging from a traditional adaptation based on the land and wine grape cultivation to the home of a university-educated couple originating from outside the Remstal. The qualitative diversity of the contemporary Burgbach population becomes evident. The chapter also expresses the major theme of continuity and change, for in the life styles of these contemporary families the long-term as well as recent adaptations of the people are revealed. In Chapter 4 we describe and interpret certain forces for cultural continuity that appear to be operating in the Remstal. We do not attempt to cover all such forces that might be relevant, rather we have selected four categories for emphasis: reaffirmation of identity, self-verifying belief patterns, ritualization, and ecological "lock-in." We must leave the meaning of these categories to the discussion in Chapter 4. In Chapter 5, *Transformation*, we are explicitly concerned with change. Much of what has been covered in other chapters has been expressive of change. In this chapter we discuss the proliferation of new business establishments and industries concomitant with the great postwar migration to the area; physical change in Burgbach reflecting both business and industrial expansion and the development of housing to meet the needs of the new population; and the effects of *Flurbereinigung* (the physical and legal reorganization of agricultural lands, particularly vineyards) on the traditional culture. We regard Flurbereinigung as a basic change, a change in principle with wide ramifications in the cultural system, in contrast to the substitutive changes in agricultural methods that we have discussed under the heading "ecological lock-in," in Chapter 4. The consequences of rationalization, as represented in Flurbereinigung and other programs sponsored by state and local governments, are touched upon in this chapter. In Chapter 6, *Schooling and the Young People*, we focus on the *Grundschule*,[4] the basic four-year elementary school to which all children go, irrespective of what channels of education and

---

[3] "We" will be used to signify the collaboration between George Spindler and the Stanford students, though the former is directly responsible for this publication.

[4] All German terms are defined in the glossary. We use certain terms because there are no exact counterparts for them in English. The *Grundschule*, for example, given its relationship to the several different educational-occupational routes possible in German society after the first four years of schooling, is not the same as "primary school" or "elementary school" in the United States. We have not followed case endings for German terms, as they would be in a German sentence, but have observed only singular versus plural, in order to reduce confusion for the English reader.

occupation they may elect later on. Here we consider the ways in which the Grundschule relates to the diversity now characterizing the Remstal population, and how the management of education within it, particularly as represented in the *Heimatkunde* (instruction about the homeland), influences choices made by young people as they mature.

We now turn to Chapter 1 and the shape of an identity.

1 / Time and land

AN IDENTITY

One of the most important public statements of idealized identity is to be found in the *Heimatbuch* (book about the homeland) published by nearly all the Remstal villages. The one for Burgbach is authored by the mayor (*Bürgermeister*) and the following three statements are drawn from it (1965:11, 12, 17).

Burgbach kann auf eine stolze geschichtliche Vergangenheit zurückblicken und ist aufs engste mit dem Ursprung des Herrscherhauses Württemberg verbunden.

(Burgbach can look back at a proud historical past and was intimately associated with the origin of the ruling house of Württemberg.)

Wie dem auch sei, soviel bleibt gewiss, dass die Herren von Burgbach von mütterlicher Seite die Ahnherrn der Wirtenberger gewesen sind und Burgbach somit mit Recht als die Wiege des Wirtenbergischen Fürstenhauses bezeichnet wird.

(Be that as it may, so much remains certain, that the lords of Burgbach have been, on the maternal side, the ancestral lords of the Wirtenberger line and that therefore Burgbach can appropriately be regarded as the cradle of the Wirtenberger princely line.)

Community identity is always based partly upon the myths of history. The villages of the Remstal each have a separate identity formed in part from the role the village is believed to have played in the long and turbulent history of the area. The passages quoted from the Burgbach Heimatbuch represent one of the most significant claims to a distinctive and proud identity by Burgbach. As the cradle of the Wirtenberger princes, Burgbach can be thought of as having been more significant during the middle medieval period than even Stuttgart or Schorndorf. This city at one end of the Remstal and this town at the other are today much larger and more urban than Burgbach. The claim that Burgbach is the "cradle" of the princes is known to every Burgbacher and to nearly all other residents of the Remstal. Although there is some ambiguity about the exact ancestral line, due to inadequate documentation for the twelfth century, the claim may be regarded as authentic. In any event, Burgbach was the seat of the counts (*Grafen*) of Württemberg[1] until the year 1321 when Count Eberhard moved the tombs of his ancestors and the endowed church (*Stiftskirche*) to Stuttgart where a better defensive position could be maintained.

Burgbach has other claims upon history as a source of identity.

> *Zu Beginn des 16. Jahrhunderts ging von Burgbach eine Bewegung aus, die alle Welt aufhorchen liess, und die bis zum heutigen Tage aufs engste mit dem Namen unserer Gemeinde verbunden ist: Der Aufstand des Armen Konrad.*

(At the beginning of the sixteenth century a movement spread out from Burgbach that all the world would hear about and that to the present day is bound with the name of our community: the Rebellion of Arme Konrad [Poor Conrad].)

Here, too, Burgbach finds its identity. In 1514 the peasants rebelled in protest against severe taxes and other forms of exploitation. The rebellion was quickly put down only to arise again a short time later, and again to be put down with severe consequences for the peasants. Although the rebellion was unsuccessful, Burgbach is defined as a place where a historically significant resistance against oppression took place.

Every school child is instructed about the history of Burgbach in the Grundschule. About one half of the Burgbacher parents migrated to Burgbach after World War II, but their children are given the content and reinforcement necessary to identify with the community. This instruction is provided in classes which have local history and ecology as their subject matter (Heimatkunde) as well as in classes devoted to religion. The following is taken from an essay written by a third grade child for her religion class about the history of the tradition-rich Protestant (*evangelisch*) church in Burgbach, usually referred to as the Stiftskirche.

> *Geschichte: Unsre Kirche, wie sie heute steht, wurde im Jahre 1522 vollendet. Diese Jahreszahl ist an einem Fenster . . .*

(History: Our church, as it stands today, was completed in the year 1522. This number can be read on a window up above the organ gallery. There must, however, have been an earlier church (or even two) here in Burgbach. The date 1416 is on one of the stones built into the base of the baptismal font, which itself must have come from an earlier church. According to an old chronicle, previously in the year 640 (A.D.) a church had been built here.

In the year 1092 our town was mentioned for the first time in history as "Burgbach." Up to this time the lords of Burgbach had made their residence up on the Kappelberg, a large hill above Burgbach. The counts of Burgbach endowed the church and established a chapter of canons to the Holy Cross, which was later expanded by Ulrich "the Thumb," the founder. Until 1321 our church remained the burial place for the count's family. Then the family cemetery lot was transferred to Stuttgart.

Earlier our church was surrounded by a high wall for defense. From this wall only a small piece with a gate tower has been preserved. Behind the church where the street is now, was the cemetery.)

There is much more in this single schoolchild's essay about the history of the church and of Burgbach. History is learned easily and becomes meaningful when

---

[1] *Wirtenberg* is the family name. *Württemberg* refers to the area.

The Stiftskirche (top) and part of the new Burgbach administrative complex (below). (Photos by Inge Schlenker (top) and Gottfried Planck (bottom), courtesy of Burgbach Administration.)

it is virtually visible to the naked eye in the stones and the structures surviving from earlier times and seen by one every day, and when it is taught by determined and skilled teachers. No child in Burgbach escapes the impact of the identity of Burgbach as it rests upon this historical base.

THE HISTORY

Burgbach history goes back far beyond the time of Poor Conrad, or even the cradling of the counts of Württemberg.[2] The Remstal was part of the northern extension of the Roman Empire into central Europe. Part of the Roman Wall lies southeast by northwest only a few kilometers from Burgbach. Its remnants can still be seen to remind one that this land has long been occupied and used. The wall was a barricade between civilization and barbarism.

The Romans introduced many cultural elements into the originally Celtic culture of the region, including the cultivation of grapes in wine making and the enjoyment of drinking wine. The evidence is sketchy but it appears that the basic ecological adaptation of the area may have had its elemental beginnings during the Roman occupation, with the population concentrated in small villages with some crop lands and possibly some vineyards. To be sure, the present relationship between village, agricultural flatland, hilly vineyards, and forest was not established until the latter part of the Middle Ages.

During the third century A.D., Germanic tribes penetrated the Roman defenses, first the Alemannen, then the Sueben, the two settling more or less peacefully in the Remstal. Roman, particularly papal, influence persisted throughout the Middle Ages in varying degrees, but political and military control of the area by Rome dissipated with the crumbling of the Empire.

We have little evidence about what happened between the third and the latter part of the fifth century when the Franks drove into the area and carried with them an interest in writing history and monks who could write it. During the next century or so, after the Franks arrived, a bureaucratic structure with a systematic tax base developed and the first fortress on the Kappelberg overlooking Burgbach was built. The so-called "half dark" age followed as the Frankish (Carolingian) Empire disintegrated during the mid-ninth century not long after Charlemagne's death.

It was during the twelfth century that Burgbach became the cradle of the lords of Württemberg and the fortress on the Kappelberg became their seat. At the same time, the Stiftskirche[3] won papal permission to hold masses and became a significant part of the religious-political structure of the loosely organized papal empire as well as the kingdom of Ulrich I. But the counts of Württemberg had consistently attempted to enlarge their realm and by that time had incurred the

[2] Sources used for this historical sketch include Marquardt (1962), Weller (1963), and Binder (1962), as well as student papers. Since literally several hundred student papers are drawn upon in this case study, none will be named specifically.
[3] A *Stift* is an endowment or grant of lands and property for a church as well as a papal permission to found a church and hold services.

enmity of several neighboring lords as well as that of the new German Kaiser, Henry VII. Enemy forces combined to invade the Württemberg lands in 1310 and destroyed the cities of Waiblingen, Schorndorf, and Rotenberg, as well as the fortress at Burgbach, much of the village, and particulary the tombs of the counts of Württemberg located in the Stiftskirche. It was then that Count Eberhard, the descendant of Ulrich I, decided to move his residence and bishopric to Stuttgart. With this, the *Glanzzeit* ("brilliant time" or "golden age") of Burgbach was over.

The destroyed fortress on the Kappelberg was never reconstructed. In 1657 there is reference to the fortress as a prominent ruin, and in 1784 it is reported that one large tower and the foundations still remained. After that time all traces of the fortress disappeared as the stones were used by the peasants as house or vineyard terrace building material. It was only recently during massive recontouring of the hillsides that the foundations of the fortress were uncovered. This discovery stimulated a rebirth of interest in Burgbach's history and contributed new materials to the Burgbach Heimat Museum and the Heimatkunde curriculum in the school.

A period of intense unrest and destruction followed with the counts of Württemberg holding off the forces of the consolidating German "Reich." The Remstal was ravaged again and again. The *Bauern*[4] were the most affected as their houses, crops, and livestock were destroyed. During the fifteenth century the lot of the Bauern became even worse. They were denied access to the forests, their taxes were raised, and weight and measure standards were devalued.

Finally, in the spring of 1514, the Bauern in Burgbach started the society of *"der arme Konrad."* As they said, as they bantered in exchanges of "gallows humor" (*Galgenhumor*), their lands lay "on hunger mountain" (*am Hungerberg*), and they were "the freemen from have-nothing" (*Freiherren von Habebnichts*) or "the princes of the empty stomach" (*Fürsten von leeren Mägen*). In the summer of 1514 the duke was surrounded by a mob of about two thousand Bauern who taunted him and hurled a few spears and rocks which rebounded off his armor. A handful of his knights rescued him and he headed for the safety of Stuttgart. But shortly after this five thousand Bauern gathered together in open rebellion. The duke returned, this time with a large contingent of knights, rounded up more than a thousand Bauern, yoked them together like cattle and held court. Ten leaders were beheaded in Schorndorf on August 7, 1514, and six more in Stuttgart two days later. The main leaders of the rebellion, however, had already fled to safer places. This was not the end of the rebellion and indeed the countryside remained in a state of unrest. The Society of Poor Conrad and the events in the Remstal became widely known as one of the first confrontations in the peasant rebellions affecting a large part of central Europe. Then years later the peasants rose again only to be put down by a better organized and more united aristocracy. Thousands fled the Remstal. This was but the first sizable out-migration that the Remstal experienced.

---

[4] *Bauer* (*Bauern*, plural) has the connotation of peasant, but today is used also to indicate farmer. "Peasant" has acquired such a complex of misconceptions and ambiguities that we prefer not to use it, and use *Bauer* instead from here on.

By then the Thirty Years War was underway and by 1634 the Austrians were marching through the Remstal, destroying village after village. After they left, only five houses remained standing in Waiblingen, a town with several thousand inhabitants. Plague and starvation broke out in the Remstal, and in many cities and villages the population was reduced by two thirds or more.

After a period of rebuilding, stability was established under an absolutistic but paternalistic rule that lasted until the beginning of the eighteenth century. The counts of Württemberg maintained an iron grip over their realm but kept the peace and developed an equitable tax structure so the Bauern could once again plow their fields and replant their destroyed vineyards. Farms prospered and cities and villages grew. But this peace, like those established previously, did not last for long. The French, between 1688 and 1693, plundered the Remstal villages and laid seige to the cities. But the seige of 1707 under the French general Villars was the last one until World War II for the inhabitants of the Remstal. The Bauern, however, did not enjoy much peace since their lords discovered that they were a valuable commodity as mercenary soldiers which could be sold to the English and Dutch. And shortly the shadow of Napoleon fell over the Remstal. As the counts of Württemberg joined Napoleon on the field of battle, the Bauern had to fight in Spain and Russia. They were among the first troops to enter Moscow and, it is said, the last to begin the catastrophic retreat during the winter of 1812–1813. When given the opportunity, the Württemberger joined with other allies against Napoleon and helped defeat the Emperor in the Battle of Leipzig.

By the time the Bauern arrived back home, however, nature had turned against them and one harvest failure followed another forcing many to leave the Remstal with their families and emigrate to America. The Remstal remained an agricultural area despite the growing pace of the Industrial Revolution which was overtaking many other parts of Europe and England.

By the middle 1860s many people of the Remstal were again caught up in the political-military maneuvering of those above them. The Württemberger at first stood against Bismarck's attempts to unify the country under Prussia and in 1866 actually went to battle against the Prussians. After the defeat of the Austrians and their allies by the Prussians, the Württemberger decided to join with the Kaiser. In 1871 the Kaiser's troops, consisting in part of troops from the Remstal, marched victoriously into Paris.

During World War I the Remstal was physically untouched but many men were lost, as the long lists of names in the churches attest. During the Nazi period the small villages of the Remstal were not a center of political action, though some of the inhabitants became Nazis. During World War II bombers passed overhead almost daily and the bombs could be heard frighteningly close as they destroyed a substantial part of Stuttgart, but Burgbach itself was untouched. The Remstal waited with great fear the coming of the French whom they thought might be the first to enter their valley. But instead, the Americans came and the postwar period began.

An enormous increase in population and great social and economic change followed shortly. Industry has come to Burgbach and only a handful of people still work the land, but the total volume of land actually worked is not much less

A Remstal village, surrounded by flatland divided into small agricultural plots, and with vineyards and orchards on the slopes. (Courtesy Don Camp.)

than it was in 1950. The population itself is no longer composed solely of *Einheimischen* (people native to the area) but rather, by about one half of its total, of people who fled the East Zone, others who were displaced from the outlying lands occupied by German minorities for centuries, and migrants from other parts of West Germany. There is also a new minority of foreigners: guest workers (*Gastarbeiter*) from Spain, Greece, Turkey, and Italy, and American students.

The village is changing physically, with 465 new buildings constructed since 1948 and 54 new business establishments. A modernistic new Catholic church stands not far from the ancient Stiftskirche. This formerly wholly Protestant village is now 22 percent Catholic. The "downtown" area has been reconstructed and a new *Rathaus* (town hall) stands opposite the towered Stiftskirche in a modernistic replication of its ancient form.

THE LAND AND ITS USES

One way of looking at any human community is through the perspective of time. Another way is from the perspective of the land and its uses.

Burgbach lies in the wide part of the Rems Valley, separated from the four other villages closest to it by distances of from one to three kilometers. As one looks from the ridge above down into Burgbach one can see the Stiftskirche and the pattern of the roofs of the older houses of the *Weingärtner*.[5] These large, usually three-storied houses shelter both humans and animals. Though compactly related to each other, they are distributed along the brook that runs through Burgbach and along what was the major north–south road to form a straggly cross (see Figure 2, p. 82). And around and between the arms of the cross are the new houses, apartment buildings and business establishments, built to house the suddenly increased population subsequent to World War II, as the great resettlement of Germany took place. The land stretches out in open space across the flat floor of the valley, distinguished by strips of various colors depending upon the crop that is planted in each strip and the stage of cultivation. On all sides of the valley rise the slopes of vineyards and orchards. The south-facing slopes are all in grape vines; the north-facing slopes more often in apple, pear, and cherry trees, and black currants. The terraced plots of vineyards are tiny, ranging in size from approximately one-twentieth to about one-half an acre. And these plots are distributed over a wide area, as owned by any single individual, so that their cultivation takes considerable moving about. On the ridges extending into the valley and along the rims of the valley itself are the remnants of the black fir forest, mixed with beech and oak. This forest, like everything else in the Remstal, is cultivated for human use. It is cut, pruned, and planted. In each forest there are a few deer and small animals, and humans can wander through it freely, as many do, every weekend.

Until World War II Burgbach and its environs was almost entirely an agricultural, folk community. Today it is a suburban community (*Vorort*) for nearby Stuttgart and other large towns in the Remstal.

This is an area of extremely high population density, about 1,000 people per square mile; a density exceeding that of the crowded rural areas of the Far East and many times higher than any comparable semirural area in the United States.

This already densely settled and much used area received a great influx of strangers at the end of World War II as refugees from the East Zone and outlying German populations as well as migrants from other parts of West Germany were resettled in Burgbach and many other small villages. The cities were in ruins and incapable of receiving them. At present, only slightly less than one half of the population of Burgbach is composed of these newcomers, together with migrants from other parts of West Germany. They brought with them different habits, different dialects, different values, and different skills. Their coming necessitated the physical expansion of Burgbach and a basic change in its social, cultural, political, and religious composition. New apartment buildings were built as quickly as possible. Burgbach extended to a little less than twice its prewar size in area covered by buildings. New industries were brought in to furnish jobs for the newcomers. A new Catholic church was built to serve the many who were not of the Protestant faith.

But Burgbach continues even into the present to be partly agricultural, partly folk, and many of its residents still think of it as a *Weinort*.[6] The *schwäbisch* dialect is still spoken within homes of the natives and often in schools when

---

[5] A *Weingärtner* is a skilled cultivator of grapes used for making wine.
[6] A village whose primary business is cultivating grapes and making wine.

An area of single-family houses and duplexes in the village. The general shape of the traditional Fachwerkhaus (upper right) is replicated in the shape of the newer houses. (Courtesy Don Camp.)

emotional or mental problems must be solved by the most efficient means of communication possible. There are fewer people engaged in growing grapes for wine and apples and pears for *Saft*,[7] but the amount of these products actually grown has not decreased. There are fewer plots in the flatland planted to grains· and vegetables for man and beast but less than 20 percent of the agricultural flatland has so far been turned to commercial or residential uses.

Burgbach is two communities; one conservative and one progressive. It is heterogeneous where it was once homogeneous. It is both a Vorort and an *ausgesprochener* (definite) Weinort. It is continuous with its own past and its own historical identity, but its future extends into an increasingly urbanized Germany. It is a place of continuity and change, where the past, present, and future are intermingled. It is this intermingling that will be described and interpreted in a preliminary fashion in the next chapter and that will be a persistent theme in the rest of the book.

---

[7] *Saft*, or juice, is made from every conceivable fruit, and is preserved for home use, sold in grocery stores, and consumed in great quantities by nearly everyone.

2 / What kinds of people are there?

A CONCEPTION OF SOCIAL STRUCTURE

Every human community consists of organized aggregates of people. These organized aggregates are formed by the application of sorting criteria that have for one reason or another become meaningful to the members of the community. These criteria may be any attribute, real or imagined, displayed by human beings. Physical attributes such as skin color, eye shape, hair form, nose shape, and body build are frequently applied. Personality traits such as aggressiveness, humor, compliance, and shrewdness may be used. Religion, family, income, education, language, skills, and ownership, all may be applied as sorting criteria. Once sorting criteria are applied and aggregates are formed, they tend to be self-perpetuating and arranged within a power and prestige structure.

The sorting criteria can be manipulated by individuals, however. They may be used instrumentally[1] to demonstrate mobility or to secure membership in prestigeful or powerful aggregates. They may also be used to demonstrate the powerlessness or defective quality of any given aggregate by members of aggregates higher in prestige and power within the system.

The application of sorting criteria within a community as these criteria and their applications evolve over time results in a social structure. As sorting criteria are applied and the aggregates thus formed are stabilized, instrumental behaviors, life goals, and life styles consolidate that are functional in each aggregate thus sorted. Peasants think and act like peasants, not lords. The social structure thus resulting contains within its very structure the sanctions for the social processes that ensure its existence. Radical alterations in conditions that challenge directly the credibility of established sorting criteria must occur before this structure will change.

A social structure is an organization of diversity. Individuals within aggregates and individuals as members of aggregates interacting with members of other aggregates are organized in their relationships. Owners and managers interact in predictable ways, *as* owners and managers with employees. They also interact, with

---

[1] By *instrumental* we refer to the use of objects, symbols, skills, and behaviors for a given end by an individual for whom that end has value.

greater but still organized variability, as representatives of different life styles, exemplified most fully in their homes and private lives. These relationships are complementary rather than simply replicative. Communities vary in the extent of the diversity that must be organized.

CHANGES IN BURGBACH

Burgbach was, before World War II, a relatively simple human community. Most of the people within it were engaged directly in an agricultural enterprise and either owned land or were related to somebody who did. They produced food and goods for their own use as well as for a market. People could be sorted on the basis of the amount of land they owned, the size of their house, the number of cattle or implements they had, perhaps even the size of the manure piles heaped up in front of their *Bauernhäuser*.[2] There were, of course, authority figures, such as the mayor, town council members, the minister, and school teachers, and there was a scattering of shop owners. But these kinds of people were in a decided minority. The business of Burgbach was land, vegetables, fruits, cows, pigs, milk, and, above all, the production of high-quality grapes for wine and the making of wine.

Today not more than 20 percent of the people in Burgbach derive any significant portion of their livelihood from agriculture. Around 50 percent derive their subsistence from industry and the remainder from community services, trade, and finance. In 1936 there were seventeen Catholics in Burgbach. The vast majority of the people were Protestant. Today there are about 1,400 Catholics in the community. In 1936 all but a tiny handful of people in Burgbach were native to the area. Today only a little more than 50 percent are native born within the Remstal, 13 percent of the population come from other parts of West Germany, 22 percent consist of those who fled from the former East Zone and outlying lands. Non-Germans constitute 10 percent. The social structure of Burgbach today is an organization of greater diversity than ever previously in its history.

Burgbach is also a much bigger community than it ever was before the war. In 1935 there were 1,600 people in Burgbach. By 1950 there were 2,537 as the population was increased by the first flood of migrants. By January 1, 1970 there were 5,003 people in Burgbach, as the process of resettlement continued to draw people to the small villages. During this period of time the "county" area (*Kreis* Waiblingen) as a whole grew by about 45 percent whereas Burgbach and many of the other villages in the Remstal tripled or quadrupled in size.[3]

This vast influx of population, bringing with it diversified attributes, has re-

2 *Bauernhäuser* (singular, *Bauernhaus*) are literally "farmers' houses," what Americans would think of as the barn—with livestock, tools, machinery, and feed—on the ground floor under the living quarters of the human inhabitants or directly adjacent to the living quarters. This term must be used rather than an English equivalent like "farmer's house" because the latter does not accurately denote the actual complex since in American imagery a "farmer's house" would be entirely detached from the barn.

3 *Kreis* is broadly equivalent to "county"; Waiblingen is the particular county in which Burgbach is located.

sulted in a complex social structure in Burgbach. New kinds of sorting criteria have become credible and have been applied, resulting in a new social structure which is a radical departure from the old.

THE NEWCOMERS

When the war finally ended in 1945 the American military government made its first assignments of 450 refugees to Burgbach. These people, virtually without possessions or funds and suffering from physical and emotional shock, had already been processed through temporary encampments set up for this purpose.[4] They were assigned as quickly as possible to existing space within Burgbach and other Remstal communities that the Third Reich had already inspected and classified while the war was still raging. Burgbach, like the other small communities of the Remstal, was virtually intact physically though its buildings had deteriorated during the years of war, and there was space and a little food. The assignment of strangers to homes, even so, was a severe displacement for both those assigned and for the people to whose homes they were assigned.

For example, in one family home, a Bauernhaus where there were cattle and pigs and chickens on the ground floor and an extended family of seven people living above them in the house, a family consisting of a man and wife and an eighteen-year-old daughter from Sudetenland (in Czechoslovakia) were assigned with three hours notice. A couple evacuated from Stuttgart had already been assigned. The two families were placed in small rooms on the third floor, vacated for them by members of the resident family. The rooms were furnished with a bed, chairs, a cot, a table, and a two-burner plate. For their room the family of three paid 12 *Deutsche Mark* per month (about $3.00 at the time). The family stayed in this room for three and a half years and then moved into an apartment. The man was employed in a nearby factory and the wife got a job in Stuttgart. The daughter finished *Gymnasium* (high school) and went on to a specialized school. During their residence in the Bauernhaus there was very little personal contact between the newcomers and the old residents. There was reserved friendliness but no intimacy. After the newcomers moved out they maintained no ties with their former hosts.

This situation was repeated hundreds of times in Burgbach. Though the established community expanded its resources to the limit to accommodate the newcomers and though the newcomers were grateful to have a secure place to stay after the trauma of having been driven from their homes, there were nearly

---

[4] It has been suggested that here, and elsewhere, I should point out the suffering that Germans inflicted upon others during World War II. I am quite aware of what the Third Reich inflicted upon Europe, and had direct experience with it as an intelligence officer in the last phases of the war in Italy. I do not, however, see this as relevant to the present analysis. The great majority of the people displaced from former German settlements of very long standing, such as the Sudetenland, and from the zone now administered by Poland, as well as those who fled from the Eastern zone (now the DDR) occupied by the Soviet Union, were ordinary men, women, and children, not Gestapo, S.S. troops, or even necessarily members of the Nazi Party.

insurmountable barriers between the newcomers and the native population. These barriers consisted of substantial differences in speech, religion, occupational and educational background, degree of urbanization, and the relationship to the land.

The newcomers were, by definition, members of a different speech community than that of their hosts. Their hosts were all schwäbisch-speaking. Schwäbisch is a speech form with a long history, a small but significant literature of its own, and several levels of social usage. It is remarkably divergent from standard High German in tonality, expressiveness, and pronunciation. Though it is a Germanic language, it is not intelligible to one who has not had long experience with it. It must, to all intents and purposes, be regarded as a separate language from High German or from the various dialects that were brought into the Remstal by the newcomers. It is true that both schwäbisch speakers and speakers of other Germanic dialects learn High German in high school. High German is, however, not truly a native language. It was created by students of language, like the Leipzig Professor Gottsched who began the ultimately accepted standardization of High German in the seventeenth century. It is not the language of intimacy in a schwäbisch-speaking community. Within the family, within the schools, within the peer group, at the taverns, the use of Schwäbisch is recognized as a membership card in the native community, the community that belongs. Of course, there is more involved than a mere dialectical difference. There is a Schwäbisch culture and character as well as a language. There are songs and jokes, pride in the slow-moving, thoughtful, shrewd character of "die dummen Schwaben" and in the schwäbisch poets and philosophers. There is what could be described as a cult of Heimat centering on the image of the cozy green valley with the little village tucked in it, safe from the outside world and irrelevant to it.

The religious difference between the newcomers and natives, represented largely in Catholic versus Protestant, may not have been as important in themselves as they might be taken to be. The Protestant sector of the community, in fact, appears to have made every effort to assimilate the new religion and its members. Space was provided from the beginning in which to hold services and by 1956 the new, very modern Catholic church had been begun with very substantial Protestant help. When the church was finished the Protestants donated a set of chimes for its tower that now ring in one-third major harmony with those of the ancient Protestant Stiftskirche. Intermarriage between the two groups began almost immediately. Of the 576 Burgbach couples married since 1945, about 20 percent represent mixed marriages. Nevertheless, for the older and most conservative members of the Protestant community the new Catholic population seemed strange, foreign, and somewhat threatening. While it may not have been a big factor in relationships between newcomers and natives, religious difference was a factor.

Possibly more important is the fact that many of the newcomers were from cities or towns of over 10,000 population and only a minority had any direct connection with the land in their home communities. This is an important difference because it leads to a different outlook. The native population of Burgbach is conservative in almost all respects. The land one owns and the crops one produces, one's bank account, the substantial possessions one owns but that do not necessarily show, are the criteria of stability and success. It is very difficult to tell who is rich and who is poor in the native tradition unless one knows the reputation of individuals.

The schwäbisch orientation is to "have it but not show it." The more urban newcomers, however, tended much more often than not to show more than they had, at least as the native population viewed them. New clothing, new cars, new apartments, new furniture were acquired as quickly as possible and, as seen by the natives, sometimes in excess of where-with-all to pay for it. An old proverb in Schwäbisch, "Schaffe, spare, Häusle baue, und sterba" (work, save, build a cottage [and a family], and die), expresses a point of view like "Bleibe im Land und nähre dich redlich" (stay home and feed yourself honestly) that is quite different than that expressed by the eager acquisition and display that seemed to characterize the newcomers, as seen by conservative natives, as they arose from the debilitated condition in which they arrived. In taste, style, and expenditures the newcomers frequently flaunted the frugal conservatism of the established citizens of Burgbach.

This confrontation and the perceptions ensuing from it were reinforced by certain material conditions. When the refugees came to Burgbach and the other Remstal communities an office was set up to establish the value of property lost by the refugee in his or her homeland and to govern compensation for it. This compensation was drawn largely from a special compensatory tax levied on privately-owned homes and business establishments. Many of the natives resented this tax and the purpose for which it was levied, even though granting that some compensation for loss had to occur. The newcomers also received favorable interest rates on building loans and ceilings were placed on rentals for rooms and apartments built by the community and occupied by the newcomers, so that apartments in Burgbach often cost about a half or even less than comparable apartments in Stuttgart. The new housing developments that were set up in rapid succession after 1948 also took land set aside by the community for other types of expansion and utilization. All of these factors contributed in some degree to a reserved if not negative attitude toward the newcomers on the part of many of the established residents of Burgbach.

The newcomers, on the other hand, had their problems of adjustment to the established citizens of Burgbach. The newcomers tended to regard the natives as *unbeweglich* (fixed, unresponsive, inflexible, unbending) and *schwerfällig* (dull, slow, sluggish, and cumbersome). The newcomers perceived the natives as hardly aware of the outside world and as displaying a strong and fixed local orientation. "The Schwaben are punished by their own existence and don't even know it," said one successful migrant. Another newcomer said, "The people here don't know what life is. They don't know how to spend money. We look and feel richer even though we have less because we know how to enjoy ourselves and spend money rather than save it."

The attitude of the newcomers to the natives was reinforced by the fact that the newcomers could not, in most cases, penetrate the land-holding membership group. Good vineyard or agricultural flatland is almost unpurchasable. Most of it exchanges hands only through inheritance or marriage. When it does sell it sells

New apartments and factories are built to accommodate the increased population. (Courtesy Don Camp.)

for a very high price, exceeding that of comparable areas in the United States. Many newcomers who wanted to buy land and become a more permanent part of the scene were unable to do so. Some felt excluded from membership in the community.

The newcomers were also frustrated by the schwäbisch speech community itself. As one newcomer said when asked whether he saw a difference between the newcomers and the natives, "Yes, when they (the Schwaben) open their mouths." Wherever the newcomers went they were reminded of the fact that they were outsiders because the people who belonged could speak to each other in a language they, the newcomers, could not understand. Perhaps this difference is accentuated and made more personally painful for some migrants because their children learned Schwäbisch from their peer group and even from the teachers within the elementary school.

Occupational differences were also substantial. Since the majority of the newcomers were not agricultural land-holders in their homelands, their occupations tend to represent greater diversification and range than those within the native population. Their skills as industrial workers and white collar and professional people changed the occupational and social structure of Burgbach virtually overnight. New factories were built in the immediate vicinity of the community. At first it was mostly migrants who worked in them. The native Schwaben were for a time left on their land but they too soon saw the advantages of a regular income, regular hours, and regular vacations. The majority of the younger generation of the established Burgbacher families have moved away from the land and toward the same occupational diversity as that represented by the newcomers.

HOW ARE THE PEOPLE SORTED?

There are many ways in which the people in Burgbach can now be sorted: people who speak Schwäbisch and people who do not; people who were born in

Burgbach of parents who came from elsewhere, and people who were born of parents whose parents and grandparents had lived in Burgbach or nearby in the Remstal; people who own land and people who do not; people who work the land and people who do not; people who have jobs in factories, and people who are skilled at various trades in varying degrees; people in white collar and semiprofessional and professional positions; people who are Catholic or Protestant, New Apostolic (*neuapostolisch*) or other; people who have higher and lower incomes; people who have more or less power; people who have more or less education; people with larger or smaller, more modern or older houses; people who seem to be more *bäuerlich* (roughly "farmerish"), or who represent more urban manners and life styles. The situation can be expressed by Figure 1.

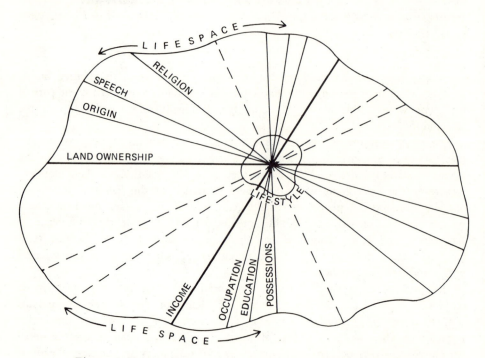

Figure 1. Vector diagram for a single individual in Burgbach.

This diagram is intended to express some of the complexity of sorting criteria as they may be applied to individuals within the contemporary Burgbach community. The sorting criteria utilize vectors that in their intersection actually determine the life style of an individual. Sorting criteria, as applied by the people living in Burgbach may utilize selected vectors, or the whole life style resulting from this intersection. Every individual has a life style different than every other individual, depending upon unique configurations of vectors. The diagram shows how the vectors may intersect for a given individual, within his or her particular life space. Vectors of greater determinant effect in the life style of this individual are represented by heavier lines. Vectors that are grouped, that is, that are more interdependent than separate, are represented by shorter distances between them along the boundaries of life space. Dotted lines represent other possible but unnamed vectors. Life space, meaning the total experience of the individual from birth to death, is represented by the outer line connecting the ends of vectors. Since no life space is a perfect circle, this one is not drawn as such. The life style changes form and quality as one moves about in one's life space through time. At any given time it is tangible and can be described.

People with similar life styles within the community constitute loose or tight social aggregates depending upon the intensity of their interaction. This interaction, in turn, is influenced by how they sort each other. Certain kinds of interactions, such as friendship and marriage, are more likely to occur within aggregates than between them. Others involving superior and subordinate relationships are more likely to occur between rather than within aggregates. One should try to imagine 5,003 such diagrams, one for each person in Burgbach, many of them overlapping but none replicating each other and all clustered into aggregates, as an abstract model of the social structure of this community. The model would be arranged sociometrically, expressing the actual network of social interaction and communication within the community. The aggregates are not abstractions, such as "the middle class," and do not have static or fixed boundaries. They are groupings of individuals and networks of relationships. These groupings reflect convergences in life styles, application of sorting criteria, and actual interactions. This model of social structure is more appropriate, we think, for urbanizing situations than a social class model. It is open-ended, accommodative, and allows for the input of new vectors and related sorting criteria that will change the system.

Some hierarchically differentiated aggregates are produced by the intersection of vectors and the application of sorting criteria. Professionals such as doctors, lawyers, and professors, and high-ranking public officers, with their greater amount of education and income, constitute a kind of top aggregate, but the technical professions (such as dentist, technical designer, and industrial chemist) and owners of substantial businesses are, in Burgbach, only slightly lower in prestige. Skilled workers and owners of small production units, such as a machine shop or small businesses, and white collar workers are not far down the scale. The relatively unskilled worker does constitute an aggregate of lower prestige but the number of truly unskilled workers within the German population of Burgbach is quite small. Most workers in Burgbach, excepting for some (not all) of the Gastarbeiter are skilled.

There are, therefore, three general aggregates sorted mainly by kind of occupation, income, and education. Professional and semiprofessional people, major public officials, and owners or managers of the larger business establishments, all with university degrees or advanced education in a technical school, constitute an upper prestige aggregate. The middle prestige aggregate consists of highly skilled workers, technical professions with intermediate educational requirements (less than a university degree), owners of small shops and production units, and regular white collar workers. The lower aggregate consists of semiskilled and unskilled workers with minimal educational achievement who are not landowners.

The ranking just described is generally applicable to the newcomers in Burgbach, and to the younger generations of natives. However, individual combinations of the vectors described result in placements within this general prestige structure that cannot be predicted. That is, the attributes of the "class" do not necessarily predict the placement of individuals on a prestige scale. Familial relationships are very important among the natives, as is land ownership (even of small pieces), participation in the schwäbisch speech community, church membership, personality characteristics, and general personal reputation and respectability.

No mention has been made of the Weingärtner as an aggregate which includes many of the older native generation. There are only about forty households in Burgbach that derive a significant portion of their income and subsistence from agricultural activities. Some of these households are among the richest in Burgbach, on the basis of ownership of land, equipment, houses, and gross income. They do not display this wealth. They tend also to represent a lower educational level than the upper prestige non-Weingärtner aggregates. Nevertheless, the Weingärtner has social standing. Weingärtner and Bauer have never meant the same thing in the Remstal. Until the beginning of the last century the Weingärtner and Bauern even lived in different kinds of houses, with the "barn" separate from the house for the former. As space became more precious, the Weingärtner

The house of a Weingärtner of the type called a Bauernhaus in this study. The livestock are kept in the area behind the manure (mist) pile, to the left of the double doors on the right.

modified their homes to include the "barn." There are about two hundred individuals in Burgbach who own vineyard plots and many of them cultivate them. Because they own land and participate in the Weingärtner pattern of symbols and behavior they have a certain position in the community, or at least among the native population, even though their other occupation and their educational level may place them in a position of relatively low prestige.

The Weingärtner tend, therefore, to constitute a separate and internally differentiated aggregate within the community of Burgbach. It is still an influential part of the community and until very recently a disproportionate number of town council members were drawn from families who have a standing within it.

Burgbach is no longer a simple folk community. It is an urbanizing community and its new diversity is an expression of the process of urbanization. It is a complex social entity, with complex sorting criteria that produce aggregates of several kinds, representing various prestige and power positions, and including different life styles. These different life styles must be given qualitative expression. In the next chapter these patterns will become clear, as the quality of life in specific households and families is described.

3 / The families

The heterogeneity and variety in contemporary Burgbach life is expressed in many dimensions. The last chapter described the kinds of people there are today in Burgbach in terms of sorting criteria such as origin, education, occupation, power, and prestige. Certain vectors converge in the life styles of individuals who then, in aggregates, create something broadly equivalent but not identical to social classes.

In this chapter we are concerned with the kinds of families there are in Burgbach. Families express the social aggregates of Burgbach in all of their various dimensions. We will describe the life styles of some selected families that express most adequately the intersection of the vectors described in Chapter 2. These descriptions are taken from student papers describing family life. They were selected from a much larger sample for their representation of the various aggregates and their life styles in Burgbach. In each case the family knew that they were the subject of a research paper and helped the student in the creation of the paper. Certain details have, of course, been altered in order to protect individuals and households. Although there are selective factors involved in which families were receptive to students, the disadvantage of selectiveness (which in some way is always present) is offset by the fact that the students could see family life from the inside. They were accepted as participants and not merely as observers. They visited their families frequently and informally over a period of some months, went with them on excursions, ate many meals with them, and participated to a surprisingly full extent in the every-day life of the family. Their major purpose in visiting the families was not to write a paper about them, but rather for friendship and to learn about German culture. This kind of entré would be very difficult to obtain under any field conditions. That it may lead to a certain idealization of the families studied seems probable.

We will begin with a young family that makes its living from the vineyards and flatland plots and that lives in a Bauernhaus. This family will represent a way of life that is disappearing rapidly from those Remstal villages closest to Stuttgart. It has strong continuity with the past. With this family as a kind of base line, we will then visit a family that contrasts with it dramatically—that of a doctor from

East Germany, a refugee, who came to the Remstal area shortly after World War II. In educational background, professional and social standing, and way of life he and his family offer the sharpest possible contrast with the Weingärtner family. The third family that we will observe is native to the Remstal but was not originally from Burgbach. The parents are three generations away from a direct connection with the land. Though schwäbisch like the Weingärtner family, they represent together with their three children a very different kind of orientation to the world about them. A fourth family that we will visit only briefly is from what is now East Berlin. They too are refugees and represent a way of life that is essentially different from the majority of the natives. A fifth family that we will encounter is native to Burgbach and but one generation away from the land, yet it represents a very modern adaptation to the Remstal environment. In this very modernity, however, we will be able to see certain continuities with the more traditional schwäbisch culture. Yet another kind of family is represented by an achievement-oriented, economically very successful family of quite a different type from any of the others. The parents were born in a large town about 30 kilometers from Burgbach within the schwäbisch-speaking culture area and moved to Burgbach during the past decade. There has been no connection with the land in their family for several generations but there has been, in their own generation, a substantial advance in social and economic position. The last family that we will visit is a family that is in transition. In one way or another, all of the families in this chapter may be considered to be in transition, just as the Remstal is as a whole. This particular family, however, is in the process of dramatic transition from a Weingärtner-tradition and land-oriented base to a modern, urban-oriented way of life. The transformation is represented in the distance between the generations within the family, and yet there is communication and continuity between them.

We will proceed inductively in the presentation of data. Interpretations and

Some people built very modern homes on the edges of the village.

generalizations will be mostly left to the end of the chapter after all of the case studies have been presented, but readers will be able to relate the various families to the framework that has been set up as they proceed.

DIE WINTER FAMILIE

Jakob and Ilse Winter are living in Jakob's grandfather's house which was first erected in the sixteenth century, though it has been modified often since. On the ground floor there are seven cows, a newly-born calf, ten chickens, seven rabbits, and two pigs. In the cellar entered from one side there are storage places for apple cider, wine, and potatoes and other root crops. In the first floor above the level where the animals live there are two bedrooms, a kitchen, and living room. The living room is well furnished with a table, comfortable chairs, a small studio couch, cabinets, and a long planter box which takes up about a fifth of the space in the room and is filled with large green plants rising to the ceiling. The bedroom in which Jakob and Ilse sleep is furnished with an enormous bed, dresser, and cupboard of light maple with fluffy *Federdecken*[1] trimmed with lace, bought by Ilse with money she saved before she was married. The kitchen is simply but adequately furnished with both a wood stove and a smaller gas stove for cooking, a sink, a small table with chairs, and cupboards. There is no running hot water, so water for dishes must be heated on the stove. There is no bathroom, though the Winters intend to install one soon. The toilet is connected to the house and has a wooden seat, a porcelain bowl, and, at the time the family was visited, no flush apparatus.[2] There is an attic over the living quarters which was never finished off with insulation or paneling so that the heavy red tile directly covers the beams and wooden cross pieces constituting the structural parts of the roof. Ilse usually hangs her wash in the attic, but since it is cold, the laundry does not dry as rapidly as she would like. She usually does her laundry at her mother's house, several doors down the street.

Thursday mornings Ilse can take her cart with its rack for pans to the community bake house, about 250 feet from her home. She enjoys these excursions very much since she can talk with neighbors and relax while her bread and *Kuchen* (coffee cake) are baking. When her lot of baking is done she will share some of it with the other women.

Jakob and Ilse work hard except on winter days. Their day begins at about five o'clock. Ilse actually gets up a bit earlier since she must make her home spotless before leaving for the fields, and the care of the livestock is one of her major responsibilities, although Jakob may prepare the cows' fodder by grinding turnips and mixing them with hay. The milk from their cows must be carried morning and night to the milk cooperative about a half a kilometer from their home. Ilse takes pride in the fact that their milk is almost the first to be delivered, and Jakob is usually standing before the door of the cooperative some minutes before it

[1] Feather-filled comforters.
[2] All houses in Burgbach now have indoor toilets that are connected to sewers and to the water system, though some do not have complete bathrooms.

opens. In the fields Ilse works very hard. At times Jakob objects that she does too much and occasionally will not allow her to do certain things that he feels are too hard.

For Jakob, much of the work is done in the same way that it was done by his grandfather and with many of the same tools. New things have been added: the tractor, electric motors to drive the press, and the grinder. But the old methods, the old tools remain; the wooden cask that holds 100 kilograms of cut grapes and that Jakob carries on his back from the Weinberge to the tractor and wagon (which may be a distance of several hundred feet) is one that his grandfather made over thirty years ago. The Winters have a four-year-old tractor which serves to pull their wagon from the Bauernhaus to the vineyard plots along with themselves and their tools. However, the tractor cannot be used for cultivation in their plots because the hills are too steep and the terraced pieces are too small. Their press used for making apple juice and pressing grapes has been recently electrified, as has the old grinder used to cut up turnips for cow fodder. Many of the hand tools, such as the several different kinds of hoes used for chopping wheat and cultivating around the roots of the grapevines, are old and were used by Jakob's father and his father before him.

The Winters do not take many trips because the cows always have to be milked and though a neighbor will step in to help, this help must be reciprocated later. Work loads differ with the season, but there is always something for them to do. Work in the vineyards is heaviest during the fall harvest. In addition to harvesting their own grapes, Jakob works at the *Kelter*[3] during this time and usually doesn't get home until two or three in the morning. After the grapes have been cut and transported to the Kelter, there is another period of hard work—the stakes and wires supporting the plants must be straightened and some replaced, the plants cut back, and the terracing walls and steps and drainage ditches repaired. In the summer months Ilse and Jakob work regardless of the weather. When snow covers the hills, they usually stay at home. There are always repairs to be made in the house and in the part of the house devoted to the livestock and equipment. New stakes have to be cut, hand equipment has to be repaired, and the livestock always need to be taken care of.

Jakob and Ilse find their work hard and their hours long, but they say they would much rather be Weingärtner than factory workers. They are, they say, independent, and they like working on the land in the open air and sunshine. But sometimes Ilse almost wishes that Jakob worked in a factory with regular hours and assured vacations. When the Winters have children as they plan to soon, Ilse's help to Jakob will be reduced significantly. This will make his work even harder.

There is little "social life" in the American sense of the word for the Winters. Their work and their families provide virtually all contact with others, excepting for that which occurs through the church. Jakob's father lives close by, as do both of Ilse's parents, and there are several aunts and uncles, Ilse's brother, and first cousins who live within the immediate vicinity. They get along well with their

---

[3] Where grapes, fresh from the vineyards, are collected and prepared for processing at the winery.

parents-in-law and spend most Sunday afternoons with Ilse's parents. Jakob would never think of spending an evening at a *Stammtisch*[4] in a neighboring tavern. To him it would be a waste of time and money, and he would not like to leave Ilse alone. The Winters do not belong to any of the numerous associations (*Vereine*[5]) in Burgbach. They say the newcomers are the ones who belong to the sport, music, or other groups. And as Ilse and Jakob say, "We can neither play an instrument nor do gymnastics, and besides, we don't need the exercise."

Neither Ilse nor Jakob are interested in music or reading. There are no books in their house, and virtually the only music they hear is that which floats in from a nearby tavern. They do not get a newspaper but usually turn on the news when it comes on the radio. They have not as yet bought a television set but they are considering it. They are in constant communication with others but their communication occurs within a fairly closed circle of rather close relatives and a few friends who are virtually like relatives. Their interests in the outside world are not intense. World and even national affairs seem beyond their horizons, though occasionally Ilse, particularly, will be attracted by a piece of news about a prominent world figure. America seems unreal and like a fairy tale to them, though they ask their student visitors many questions about it.

Entrenched as they are in the traditional ways of Burgbach, the Winters are tolerant of the new elements which have moved into town, sympathizing with the refugees from the East Zone who have settled in Burgbach. The only word that Ilse has ever said against them was that it was too bad that the Catholics among them were able to alter the annual *Kirbe* (see p. 54 and glossary) celebrations because one of them fell on a Catholic holiday. Though the Winters disapprove of the Catholic Church somewhat because of some of its doctrines, they believe that all religions have a good effect on people. They think it right that the community should have done everything possible to see that the Catholics have their own church. They are also tolerant of the Gastarbeiter, mostly Greek, who have come to live in Burgbach. As Jakob says, "There is a labor shortage in Germany, and unemployment in Greece, so the workers have every right to come here." And, "After all, they need bread to live, too."

The Sunday routine begins for the Winters the same as any other day—the cows must first be milked. After breakfast they change into their Sunday clothes and go to the Protestant Church. Although they attend church regularly, they are not noticeably religious as far as any specific observances the rest of the week. After church they eat dinner and then they go to visit Ilse's parents where they stay until about five o'clock when it is time for the cows to be milked. Then Sunday is over.

The Winters' life goes on in much the same pattern from year to year and in much the same way as it did for their parents and grandparents. The size of the grape harvest each year is important, as is being first in line to turn in the milk at the cooperative and always having clean front steps and a clean, decent house.

---

[4] A table at a local tavern reserved for a regular group who meet there to drink, talk, and sometimes sing.

[5] The *Vereine* are somewhat formalized interest or hobby groups that meet and carry on activities more or less regularly.

There are dreams of far off places like America but much closer to their reality is the old schwäbisch saying, "Work, work, save, save, build a house, lie down, stretch out your feet, and die." The Winters are saving. Their bank account is growing each year and is now probably larger than that of many of their more urbanized neighbors in Burgbach. They do not believe in showing everything that they have or of making a show of anything. They are planning ahead for the improvement of their old but comfortable and basically efficient house, the purchase of new equipment, children, a car, and possibly even someday purchasing some more land. The latter is less likely than anything else. Land is almost impossible to buy. Not only is it extremely expensive, but most people do not like to give it up. They see, however, in the coming *Flurbereinigung*[6] some possibilities, for there may be some people with only a small piece of vineyard who will be interested in selling.

Neither Jakob nor Ilse have the advanced technical or literary education to do anything else other than what they are doing, but also they are deeply steeped in the traditional values that make working the land something of high value. And they have both learned a great deal about growing grapes for production of wine, a complicated profession.

DIE SCHMID FAMILIE

Herr Dr. Schmid settled in Burgbach after his flight from East Berlin and married a young woman from the vicinity but not from Burgbach, who had been forced to leave Sudetenland in Czechoslovakia as a child with her family at the end of the war. The Schmids own a substantial single-family dwelling built only three years ago. Before that they had lived in a much older but comfortable single-family house. There are four children: a boy of twenty-two, now in the army, a boy of eighteen, a girl of fifteen, and a boy of thirteen, all attending the Gymnasium and living at home.

The father is distant and formal with the children. When they gather for dinner at night, he asks each one in turn about his or her homework, and when that is done, turns to other matters. Frequently he has a meat dish while other members of the family will have something else, since he works hard as an official for the county medical services. Almost every night he practices on his violin in the wood-paneled living room. The family leaves the room so as to not disturb him. When guests come to the house and particularly when there is a gathering of two or three other musicians, the father will be joined by his 18-year-old son who is becoming very proficient on the viola. If a formal practice session is to be held, the guests are given something to read but cautioned not to rustle the pages as they turn them. Half way through the evening there will be a pause of 15 minutes during which free social interaction may take place and some refreshments may be taken.

The children spend a great deal of their time at home, but much of this time is spent on schoolwork. The parents are very concerned about their getting the

---

[6] A process of vineyard and other small plot consolidation in both physical and legal dimensions that will be discussed at length in Chapter 5.

schoolwork done. The father confines his interest mostly to asking whether the homework is done and berating anyone who does not finish it promptly. The mother is sympathetic to the children and tries to help them with their homework when they get stuck. She also tries to mediate between the children and the father by solving problems before they come to his attention, and hustling the children out of the room when a dispute begins to arise. The mother gives the impression of being affectionate but nervous. She tries to please both the father and the children simultaneously and sometimes their purposes are at odds.

The eighteen-year-old son models himself after the father. There was a time when he resented him, but now he sees him as an excellent man and one to be emulated. He accepts his father's exacting tutelage on the viola and will play passages over and over again until they meet his father's high standards. He says that he anticipates reaching concert standard, though music will always remain a hobby for him. He intends to become a university professor in languages. When he is talking to Americans he sometimes feels a little embarrassed about his own expressions of confidence and attempts mannerisms suggesting modesty which he learned as an exchange student in an American high school. This is a simulated posture, however, for him.

The oldest daughter models after the mother. She is warmer and generally easier going than her older brother. She and her mother are quite close and give each other emotional support. The youngest son and the father are at odds with each other. He does least well of all of the children in the exacting lessons of the Gymnasium,[7] and at the moment is failing in mathematics. His mother is trying to help him in this but the matter has come to the attention of his father who continues to make demands that he do better. Whereas the older son is clearly modeling himself on his father's behavior, the younger boy seems to be increasingly hostile and rejective, and appears to be developing into a rebel.

The aspiration level of the family is high. It is expected that each of the children will go into one of the professions, and given the requirements of a German professional education, the preparation begins far down in the school years. It is not strange then that schoolwork is a major preoccupation within the family.

The children appear to have few friends and cannot be said to be members of a peer group in the same sense that American children would. They go to school and after school come back home, often to begin their homework as soon as they arrive. Television viewing time and program selection is strictly controlled, even for the oldest boy. Each of the children has some outside association in a group of an interest-centered nature such as a Musikverein. Participation is limited, however, to specific meetings with a definite time duration. The parents, at least the mother, know at all times where each child is and when he or she will return. Evenings are spent with the children doing their homework, the father practicing on his violin, and the mother sewing, knitting or reading, or helping the children with their homework. When television is watched it is for a specific program and the set is turned off between such occasions.

---

[7] The Gymnasium is one of three major types of school to which children go after elementary school. A Gymnasium education leads to the university and the professions and is the most difficult academically.

Books and magazines of high quality are visible here and there about the house. The parents deplore the tendency of the popular German magazines to concentrate on "cheap publicity" about famous people and exposure of the nude female body. The magazines they have in their home are not of this type. The parents and sometimes the family as a whole go to the symphony, opera, ballet, and theater quite frequently, and this constitutes a major recreational outlet. The family has not been able to take a vacation together for the last few years because the father has been so busy. But the mother and the three children went to the North Sea for a vacation last summer.

The family is not religious and does not attend church. They do not, however, denigrate those who do.

Their attitude toward the native Schwaben may be said to be essentially neutral. They find the Schwäbisch speech impossible to understand when spoken in its deepest *bäurlichen* (rustic) accent, and they ascribe certain personality and intellectual characteristics to the Schwaben which are neither entirely complementary nor entirely negative. They think of the less educated Schwaben as "slow, shrewd, and limited." They do, however, recognize differences between various aggregates of the native born and avoid lumping them all together. People like the Winters, however, would be beyond their frame of reference. While they would respect the Winters as hard-working, respectable people, there would be no thought of any direct association with them on any kind of social basis. The family culture and general life style of the Schmids is as foreign to that of the Winters, and vice versa, as any two cultural variants within the Western framework could be, even though they are both German and live in a community of around 5,000 people.

DIE SCHLEINER FAMILIE

The Schleiners are natives who live in Burgbach but were born elsewhere in the Remstal. They live in a duplex, occupying both a ground floor and a first floor above. They are Schwaben but third generation away from the land. Herr Schleiner is a white-collar worker at an intermediate technical level in a large machine tool factory in Stuttgart. He has no university degree but has gone through four years of *Fachschule* (technical school) beyond the *Realschule*.[8] Frau Schleiner is not as well educated as her husband, having had eight years of nonspecialized schooling which she finished at fourteen, and three years of training in home economics intended as preparation for the housewife's role rather than as preparation leading to an advanced degree. They have three children, a boy of sixteen and another of fourteen, and a girl of eleven.

Herr Schleiner is forty-eight years old, active and vigorous, and unusually tall and slim. He exhibits a very active interest in whatever he is talking about and what is going on about him. He always wants to know where any place is located to which a student refers and will light up a large world globe in the living room

---

[8] The school that ranks between the Gymnasium and the Hauptschule in academic orientation. Children go there after completing elementary school (Grundschule).

to check to see. If a subject comes up about which he is uninformed, he will go to one of the several large reference books and look up the subject. For instance, in one conversation the difference between crocodiles and alligators came up. He looked up these animals in his large zoological encyclopedia and read the appropriate sections out loud.

The mother, Frau Schleiner, is about forty years old and is short and much heavier than her husband. She is very much the housewife, staying home most of the day to knit, cook, and clean. She is a calm and pleasant person, and extends an open and comfortable hospitality to visitors. She rarely takes a particularly active part in the conversation, though she will enter in when something interests her. She is always busy, knitting sweaters, socks, hats, vests, gifts for relatives, and other useful articles. If she is not knitting or sewing, she is cooking or cleaning. The house is always perfectly cleaned and straightened up. She is aided in her effort to maintain a perfect house by her family. No one ever leaves things lying about or tracks in dirt. Everyone changes from street shoes to slippers at the front door. Frau Schleiner is the authority on what the children are doing, how the relatives are, and what the family did. On these matters she will correct her husband when he is wrong. On matters not directly connected with the families' activities, however, such as draft laws, places to go for the weekend, or President Nixon's popularity in America, she does not have much to say.

Each member of the family has a distinctive personality and is treated as such by the other members. The parents have very clear-cut concepts of each child's abilities and limitations. They think of the oldest child, a Gymnasium student, as extremely intelligent and quiet. They feel that he definitely will go into a profession and is the "student" in the family. The younger boy they characterize as easy going and more physical. He is already beginning to be quite an athlete, and is attending *Realschule* at present, which will not lead him to one of the professions. He definitely does not want to go to school any longer than he has to, and there seems to be no question in anybody's mind that he should. He does not know what he wants to do as an occupation, nor is there very much pressure on him to make up his mind at present, though the parents are concerned. They praise his athletic achievements and avoid comparing his relatively mediocre school performance with that of his older brother. The youngest girl is the darling of the family. Cute and talkative, she sometimes occupies the center of the stage, but not for too long. Herr and Frau Schleiner do not let her get out of hand. For any misbehavior or impoliteness they immediately reprimand her, and she seems to feel that they definitely mean it. When she was late to school one day Frau Schleiner quizzed her for about five minutes on whether or not she apologized to the teacher and warned her to never again take so long getting ready. When Herr Schleiner came home he gave her another verbal going over. She is not as good a student as her older brother nor as well organized as her middle brother and tends to be somewhat of a procrastinator. Her parents try to correct this but avoid a high emotional intensity in their efforts. They feel that there is no particular point in her going to the Gymnasium, and as a matter of fact, that such an education is somewhat irrelevant for girls anyway.

Each of the children has a definite personality and role within the family. Each has their abilities and inadequacies. These all appear to be accepted as givens and with complacency.

The most important aspect of the child-parent relations, as seen from the American perspective, is the very close supervision of all of the children's activities by the parents. Herr and Frau Schleiner know exactly where each child is at any given time, what the status of the child's work at school is, and what their problems are. The family is extremely close-knit as seen from the American observer's perspective, and spends a great deal more time together than a comparable family unit in America. During a period of contact lasting for six months, there were very few children brought into the household by any one of the three offspring. Though they were apparently in good standing with their peers and have what was regarded as a satisfactory social life, this did not mean an active peer group association or any constant running through the house or using household facilities for parties or group meetings. In fact, there was very little time in which these things could happen since the children would go to school and then come home to help with some minor household chore and to do their homework almost every day. When there was free time, the entire family would take a trip, and each summer the family plans together a longer trip of a couple of weeks to some interesting place in Italy, Spain, or Scandinavia.

The use of space within the home is relevant as an attribute of life style. All of the rooms in the Schleiner's half of the building are, by American middle class standards, quite small, with a living room approximately 11 by 15, a parents' bedroom about 9 by 11, a kitchen 8 by 12, a children's bedroom of 12 by 13. There are an electric, three-burner stove, a small refrigerator, and an oven in the kitchen. The refrigerator, though small, is still almost always empty, holding perhaps one or two leftovers with a few things like mayonnaise, mustard, and a quart of milk. Frau Schleiner, like most housewives in Burgbach, shops every day for supplies. The sink is not made of porcelain but of a brown plastic material. There is no running hot water and there are no electric mixers, electric knives, blenders, or other mechanized equipment in the kitchen. Frau Schleiner says that things do not taste as good unless they are made strictly by hand. She prides herself on her handmade noodles and Kuchen which she bakes in her own oven rather than in the communal bake house.

The children's bedroom is always neatly kept. The bunk beds are covered with colorful Federdecken. The room also contains tables, a couch, and three dressers. All three children use the same room and all their belongings are stored there. The walls are covered with shelves for books and toys, pictures, and framed sports certificates. The daughter's chrome-trimmed doll carriage is kept in one corner. Everything else is neatly tucked away under the beds or behind the door. The room is quite cold in winter because the door is usually shut and only those rooms that have to be warm are heated, as is most often the custom except among rich people. The parents' bedroom is not luxuriously furnished but has comfortable twin-sized beds placed next to each other and covered with both blankets and Federdecken. The room is very cold because the door is always kept shut.

The living room is indeed the room where people live within the home. There is space for each activity and one source of heat, a small stove into which a lump of coal and burnable trash is put. This, besides the heat coming from the stove in the kitchen, constitutes the source of heat for the living quarters. There is a glass-covered sideboard filled with dishes, souvenirs, whatnots, and some ceramic articles made by the children in school. There are pictures of relatives, including several killed in the war. The dining table is in the corner, covered with oilcloth for meals and there is a coffee table on which there are usually copies of *Moderne Frau* and *Constanze*, both respectable magazines. In another corner there is a record player-radio with a world globe on top. There are comfortable chairs, two large chests in which a variety of household articles are kept, and a Chinese screen that the Schleiners were given for Christmas. The wall opposite the door boasts a large picture window with white lace curtains and the usual heavy outside blinds that can be let down from inside each evening. Growing on each side of the window are banana plants whose roots are in a long planter which covers the entire side of the room where the window is. Plants are in all the other rooms including the bedrooms and the kitchen, usually on the window sills, sometimes on the tables or shelves.

The bathroom has yellow fixtures and pretty towels, soap, and a box of cosmetics. Although the bathroom is not large, it also contains the washing machine and some of the family's clothes are hung there. There is a bathtub with a shower attachment. Water is heated once a week for baths and washing clothes.

The American observers were always impressed with how neat and uncluttered the living quarters were kept despite the fact that they were used by five people with diverse interests. Everything is put away after it is used. Nothing is left lying about. This orderliness seems to be as natural for the children in this family as disorderly carelessness seems to be for many American children.

The Schleiners know the families living in close proximity to them but are only on friendly speaking terms with them. Their family ties are, however, very close. They talk about relatives, have pictures of them, and visit them often. The family is content to spend its evenings at home together, gathered in the living room, carrying on individual activities. They do not have a television set, feeling that it is an intrusive element that they would rather not have. The children do, however, go over to the home of Frau Schleiner's parents a few blocks away to look at television, once or twice a week, for specific programs.

By the standards of the American student observers, the family was frugal in its expenditures and use of space and materials. Leftovers simply do not exist at meals because everything that is served is eaten. If there are any leftovers at all, they are consumed later. Lights are turned off in any room that is not being used at the moment. There is no phone, as the Schleiners regard this as unnecessary. As reported previously, only the living room and kitchen are heated. The other rooms get some heat from the warmth of the adjacent walls but have none of their own, and by American standards could not be regarded as anything less than very cold, from November through April. The stairwell, entry hall, and other similar space, are also entirely unheated. And yet, in no sense can the family be said to be living at a substandard level. The members of the family are all well clothed, well fed, have recreation, and own toys as well as all necessary implements. As the Schleiners say of themselves, "We think our life is a good one."

DIE WEIS FAMILIE

Herr and Frau Weis are both from Berlin and moved to the Remstal area in 1946. They are both university educated and Herr Weis is with the Baden-Württemberg land-use planning office. A son, twenty-two, is studying to be an architect, and a daughter, nineteen, to be a teacher. Neither one lives at home at present, though both come home weekends and vacations whenever possible. The family lives in a pleasant first-story apartment, well furnished and with modern appliances. We will provide only a vignette to demonstrate a variety of inner-family life that is frequently encountered at this socioeconomic and professional level.

The Weises are always interested in something. At the moment it is the discovery of a piece of Roman sculpture in a sewer ditch that is being dug in the area. The son and daughter, both home for the weekend, get very excited about the possibility that no one will take an accurate recording of the site so that the dating of the find and the determination of its significance may be impossible. Concern over this escalates during dinner to the point where finally Herr Weis calls the Superintendent of Excavations and Street Repair on the phone (at 11:00 P.M.!) and tries to get from him an assurance that attention will be paid to the find. After a long and increasingly intense conversation the superintendent does agree to the request that experts be called in.

The conversation then shifts to certain prehistoric sites visited by the family on recent trips to France. The children and the parents all become extremely involved. Voices rise as disagreements about the location or specific character of sites are generated, but there is no ill-humor. Their preoccupation is such that the guests present almost drop out of sight and mind.

After dinner things quiet down a bit and the family turns its attention to a wide-ranging series of engagements with the outside world. Politics, artistic events, philosophy, psychoanalysis and its recent twists and turns are all subjects for discussion.

At the same time there is a kind of intense affective interrelationship between the children and the parents, but particularly the mother. Both of the children must leave early in the morning to go back to school. The mother is asking questions about whether or not they have plenty of clean clothes, what they are doing with their evenings, what their friends are like. The children answer without seeming resentment. There are many open displays of affection. Apparently a very maternal relationship exists between the mother and both children, though perhaps more intensely with the son.

The children come home from school whenever possible and stay with the family as long as possible. All vacations are still taken together. Plans are being made for next summer. One has the feeling that other places, other people, other events are secondary to the family and its inner life. The family has an internal relevance and validity that may seem to be lacking in the outer society. Home and family are real and exciting. It is within this context that the Weises are most fully themselves. The world may be harsh, impersonal, and irrelevant to personal wishes, but the inner world can be manipulated. It is a warm, affectionate, supportive atmosphere.

These two qualities characterize this home most fully: the intense, excited concern with intellectual matters; the warmth, security, and interpersonal recognition within the family.

DIE SCHWAB FAMILIE

The Walter Schwab family lives in a pleasant single-family house on the outskirts of Burgbach close to the church where they attend services. In front of the house there is a small garden in which vegetables, herbs, and flowers are grown. To the left is a small garage which houses their 1967 Opel. On the right there is a wooden shed in which bicycles and tools are kept. The backyard is large enough for the boys to play ball in, for outdoor gatherings, and for a badminton net. There are several fruit trees, shrubs, and flowers that bloom profusely in the spring. In addition, rabbits are kept in a wooden pen.

To reach the door of the house one must climb some steps. As the doorbell is rung, a member of the family goes to the window above the door, opens the window, and looks out to see who is calling. Only then will the door be opened. It is always kept locked, as is the custom in Burgbach despite a low, almost nonexistent crime rate. In the winter as one climbs the stairs to the second floor, one notices the coldness in the cement stairwell. As usual, there is no central heating.

The nature of the space available and its use is broadly similar to that of the Schleiner family. The bedrooms are not heated and one depends on the heavy Federdecken to keep one warm at night. There is a bathroom and modern toilet, a wash basin with only cold water and a small gas heater and a bath tub. The living room is closed off from the hall by a door which is almost always kept shut during the winter to keep in the heat. The room area has a coal or wood-burning stove for heat. Green plants cover almost one entire wall. There is a radio-phonograph console, a sewing machine, a large chest of drawers, a clothes hamper, and in the middle of the room a large square table used for many of the family's activities such as sewing, reading, knitting, conversation, and eating. The glassed-in standing cupboard holds knickknacks and gifts, souvenirs of trips, and some fine chinaware. The two boys, twelve and nine, sleep in a room on the first floor which is unheated. The basement below them is used to store tools and is cool enough to store eggs, beer, and fruit. There is also a freezer and a cider-making apparatus in the basement.

Herr Schwab works as a foreman in a factory that produces women's sandals and he has about twenty-five employees under his supervision. Frau Schwab does not work at present, though she did several years ago.

The Schwabs own a plot of land amounting to about a fifth of an acre on which they grow strawberries, raspberries, red currants, sour cherries, potatoes, salad greens, carrots, kohlrabi, cucumbers, and garden herbs. On this land they grow most of the vegetables and fruit that they consume during the summer and a substantial portion, preserved by both freezing and canning, that they consume in the winter.

They also own fifteen rabbits which they keep in the backyard pen. The rabbits are an important source of protein for the family and are cooked in a variety of ways. The Schwabs also make their own Saft (juice) from cherries, apples, and raspberries, and a kind of hard apple cider called *Most*.

A meal at their house is always delicious. Homemade *Apfelsaft* may be the beverage. There will be warm potato salad made with Frau Schwab's homemade mayonnaise. And there will be homegrown cucumbers, homegrown salad with oil and vinegar, rabbit legs and gravy, steamed homegrown potatoes, and cream pudding.

Frau Schwab makes some of the clothes for the family and does quite a bit of knitting. The Schwab family produces a lot of its own food and Frau Schwab stretches the family budget further by very careful buying. She knows just where to obtain the best bargains in food and clothing in the various stores, whether in Burgbach or in larger towns not far off. The members of the Schwab family are careful about other kinds of expenditures as well. Lights are turned off. Heat is conserved, and only as much hot water is used as is needed for cleanliness. But the frugality is not merely for its own sake. They save for vacations, for a new car, and for remodeling their house. All of these things will be done with great care and forethought and little display.

The older boy is a student in the Realschule. There he studies English, mathematics, chemistry, German, composition, and history. Twice a week he has religion classes, and once a week a citizenship class. He has four more years in the Realschule and then must complete an examination. Perhaps then he will go on to a specialized school and might even become an engineer, but is likely to settle for a more modest technical level. The younger boy attends Grundschule. He is studying the same subjects that his older brother is but at an elementary level. He is preparing for a two-day examination that will determine whether or not he is eligible to attend Realschule. These are anxious days. The exam is mostly in mathematics and science. The examination for the Realschule is hard enough. No one in the family is thinking seriously about Gymnasium for either of the two boys. Not everybody wants to be a professor, a lawyer, or a doctor, the Schwabs say.

The boys have their friends at school. Though they play with them outdoors, they are rarely together in the house. The two Schwab boys are good friends with each other and spend a large part of their free time in each other's company. Both of them a have a lot of homework to do, and this plus various family activities keeps them at home for a considerable amount of the time that they are not in school. The boys are closely supervised by their parents. "Smart" behavior is not tolerated, though the Schwabs cannot be considered authoritarian with their children. When one of the boys comes home to tell his mother that he has smoked two cigarettes with a friend, her reaction is practical. She tells him how bad it is for his health, but she does not seem upset by it. Every week the boys receive a modest allowance, somewhat smaller than most of their friends. Occasionally they also receive small amounts of money for help about the house. The boys sometimes roughhouse at home. If things start to get out of hand, the father will speak to them. Once when they did not desist immediately, he gave them both a good-natured but very solid whack. They stopped at once, but there was no emotional upset. The boys do not have too many chores. They keep their rooms in order, and once in a while feed the rabbits. However, Frau Schwab cleans the house, keeps it in excellent order, and seldom requires any help from anyone. The boys see their home as a good place and their parents as lovable people.

The Schwab family's main activity is the evangelische Kirche. The whole family attends almost every Sunday, and Frau Schwab is a member of the Women's Auxiliary Organization. Religious observances are carried into the home for religious holidays and grace is said before every meal. The boys attend Sunday School as well as a Youth Group meeting; Frau Schwab sings in the choir; and both Herr and Frau Schwab attend a Bible class. The family does not have many other activities but visit their nearby relatives often and have a sense of family unity.

Most of the people whom the Schwabs see speak the schwäbisch dialect. They also speak it in their home and with the children, as is the case with most schwäbisch-speaking families. The Schwabs feel that the language itself gives one a sense of relationship to those who also speak it.

The Schwab family has made an adaptation to contemporary reality that reflects the modernization of the Remstal. They are not tied to the land like the Winter family, and yet there are some things that show that the Schwabs are native to the area. The land is used by them to raise food that they would otherwise have to buy and the work they do on it is valued. They also express in other ways certain values that can be thought of as traditional in the Remstal area. Their thrift, their careful utilization of their resources, their use of money to improve the substantial aspects of their existence rather than its more showy aspects, their careful appraisal of relevant aspirations appear to represent the cautious world view of the Schwaben. And like other families, they seem to operate in a relatively closed circle of friends and associations, with the home and family as a center of activity.

DIE LOCHER FAMILIE

Both Frau and Herr Locher were born in a nearby city close to the Remstal. Herr Locher is a manager of a large bottling works near Burgbach. They moved from the city to Burgbach to be closer to his work so he would not have to commute. The Lochers own a large apartment house in Stuttgart and have just recently built a large single-family house in Burgbach. Their two sons are in the Gymnasium and have high-level business or professional careers ahead of them. The family may be considered urban einheimisch.[9]

[9] There are times when "Schwaben" or "native" does not fit the case. The Lochers are native to the area but their grandparents were not Schwaben. They are "native" (born in) Baden-Württemberg, but "native" is less appropriate than "einheimisch" in their case.

Things were not always so good for the Lochers. Herr Locher's father was a shoemaker and though he made a reasonable income from his work, the family of eight in which Herr Locher grew up was never well-to-do. Frau Locher had been a cook's apprentice for several years and her father had been a semi-skilled machine worker, with a large family to support.

The years following the war were hard for the Lochers, but the "economic miracle" (*Wirtschaftswunder*) that later overtook Germany overtook the Lochers as well. Although Herr Locher did not have the usual background for such a high-level position, he rose rapidly to prominence in the managerial group of the bottling works.

Their new house cost over 300,000 D.M. (about $86,000) to build (in 1967), not including the purchase of the property upon which it stands. At least 6,000 D.M. ($1,660) more must be added to that for landscaping. The house is very similar to a typical upper-middle class American home in suburbia though brick, concrete, and stone are used rather than wood for building materials. The house and furnishings are very modern, and the interior decoration is done in a modern provincial style. All the floors except the basement, kitchen, and bathroom have wall-to-wall carpeting. The windows are large and spacious. The kitchen is equipped with an automatic dishwasher, bread cutter, deep freeze, electric chopper, and a mixer. The dining room, entry hall, the writing and telephone room, the living room (with TV), the hobby room, and master bedroom and bath complete the layout on the first floor. There is a paved patio and garden decorated with cast-iron lawn furniture. In the upper level of the house there are three bedrooms, a lounge, storage space, and a bathroom with shower. The basement is fully equipped for washing, drying, and ironing, and contains a modern central heating unit.

The house is very important to the Lochers and figures largely in many of their conversations. Should those flowers be moved to the other side of the house? Why is the enamel in the bathroom no longer as shiny as it was? How should the carpet be cleaned? It's about time to have the windows washed! That picture really doesn't do well on that wall!

In general, material and physical comfort are high on the priority list fot the Locher family. The house itself reflects this priority, so do their two cars, both expensive and new. They eat very well also. They have beef, lamb, pork, or even steak at 10 D.M./500 gr. ($3.60 for 1.1 pound), or chicken, which is not cheap in Germany. For breakfast there is usually coffee, which is approximately four times more expensive in Germany than in the United States, soft-boiled or scrambled eggs, several kinds of rolls and bread with butter, a variety of jams and jellies, cold cuts, and several kinds of cheese. This menu contrasts very sharply with what is usually eaten by the families whom we have described, and is a departure from the diet of most other relatively well-to-do families.

Frau Locher has a large collection of glassware and dishes. She takes pride in them and points out that there has to be a different glass for everything.

One cannot really drink coffee out of a teacup, or wine from a milk glass. To the young, they all taste the same, but to a knowledgeable person (a *Kenner*), it does not taste good if you drink it from the wrong glass or cup. Why do you think there are different glasses and forks and spoons for everything? It is culture. To be sure there are people in Burgbach who even eat the food out of the paper it comes in, but even when our boys go camping they take along different pots and pans for serving, a matching tea service and coffee service and cooking utensils, serving utensils and other things to eat with properly. Food should be well prepared and also nicely served. We always try to see to that.

Frau Locher believes that material comfort is important and feels that it is also important for her children and their future. She commented on her son:

He wants a wife to make him good things to eat. He needs a job to bring in money. He wants to have a nice car, to eat well, live comfortably, and have a little plesaure. That's really all there is in life.

Money is a means for getting the good things in life. "When you want something good, you have to pay for it," Herr Locher says. Money is an important topic of conversation in the household. References are made to the cost of the house, the garden, the Mercedes, the vacation trips, and various articles about the house such as the typewriter, the dishwasher, and the dryer. Other people, as well, are often evaluated by how much they own and how much they may have spent to obtain what they have.

The Locher family is concerned with status. Status is exemplified by the size of one's house and the quality and style of one's possessions. Frau Locher is very concerned about keeping the house immaculate, setting out the right kind of lawn furniture, arranging the walk up to the house in the best way, matching the flowers to the furniture and the trim of the house.

After visiting one of the neighbors in Burgbach who had just completed a new house, Frau Locher became dissatisfied with her own beautiful living room. She felt that the neighbor's rug was thicker and the room more nicely laid out. She began to talk about the time when they could have their house redecorated, even though at that time it was only a year-and-a-half old.

The Lochers feel that work and a dedication to work is all-important. Frau Locher talks about all the work she does (housecleaning, baking, ironing, shopping), and expects her boys to help. She says young people must be "hilfsbereit" (ready to help). Herr Locher proudly states that he has gotten where he is mainly by hard work. He says he never thought of anything but his work for years. And even today he is at the office at eight o'clock and rarely comes home until well after six in the evening.

Both Herr and Frau Locher feel that education should be practical and prepare one for an occupation. She says, " 'Die ewigen Studenten' (eternal students) who read and think too much, never have a well established job. They are not even responsible enough to raise their own families." She feels that it is the parents' responsibility to educate their children so that they can get good-paying jobs.

Cleanliness and order are important values and are standards for judging other people as well. Frau Locher asks the boys when they come back from other homes, "Does she keep a clean house? Was there any clutter?"

Predictability and planning are important. She criticizes others who do not appear to have definite plans. She expects her boys to have a definite daily plan. At breakfast she asks them what they will do that day, and they outline hours of study, work, and letter-writing. She is irritated when they do not seem to have a definite plan.

Privacy and the family group itself appear to be two positive values for the Lochers. Family interaction tends to be limited to close friends and a few relatives. The Lochers do not know many people in Burgbach, and have their most intimate associations with people who live in Stuttgart and Esslingen, two nearby, large cities. The house itself reflects a desire for personal privacy. There are many different rooms in the house and specific activities can be carried on in these different rooms. TV watching occurs in the living room, while writing or studying takes place in the boys' rooms or at the writing table downstairs.

Frau Locher tends to have a careful attitude toward outsiders. She feels at times that they may be trying to take advantage of her family because they are better off than many others and live in a nicer home. She feels also that tradesmen may sometimes try to charge them too much for the same reasons. She does not engage in conversation easily with strangers and is fairly perfunctory in her relations with neighbors. Despite their pride in the home, the Lochers have few people in for dinner, coffee, or cocktails.

The boys have friends in the Gymnasium, but virtually never bring anyone to their home, nor do they visit anyone else's homes. The family has taken most of their vacations together and when they have not, the boys have gone without anyone else along. The parents want to know exactly where the boys are at any time. The older boy went to a party that lasted until three o'clock in the morning. Frau Locher said that that will never happen again. "We are responsible parents and we will see to it." The boys spend considerable time at home, helping around the place, even helping Frau Locher wash clothes and do housecleaning. Both play musical instruments which takes up some of their time. Little reading is done in the home besides schoolwork, though the family takes several magazines, including *Der Spiegel*, and the Stuttgart newspaper. Selected programs are watched on television but it is never left to run on unattended or casually.

Frau Locher dominates conversations and is emphatic about expressing her opinions. Since Herr Locher is almost always at the office, family life tends to revolve around her. Herr Locher, however, does not believe that his wife has the major decision-making role in the family, although he regards her as an equal partner in the decision-making process. He says, "Both a man and his wife are the head of the family. The husband should even help his wife with her housework, if necessary. Housework does not destroy manliness." And further, "The man should make decisions about financing, house-building, and see that the outside equipment and cars are in good condition. The woman naturally makes decisions about the interior of the house. She is the one who has to take care of it." Concerning decisions about family plans, he says, "Both the man and wife should make decisions after discussing the problem. If one of us thinks we should do one thing and the other something else, we talk over the advantages and disadvantages of both plans and then decide. Today it is no longer true that a man stands at the head of his family in all things." In actual practice, the Lochers seem to work it out this way. It is true, however, that occasionally it appears that Herr Locher has the final say. Sometimes, it seems to him, his wife is distracted by irrelevant details and that his judgment is better. When this is so, he does not hesitate to act as the final authority.

The Lochers represent a family type that is different from the others in our selected group. Possibly some of their concern with material things is a result of the deprivation and then the abundance that they experienced because of the ups and downs in Germany during the last several decades. However, even though they have a larger house and more money to spend than their einheimisch acquaintances, they exhibit many of the same general values. Although they have ample space and a variety of rooms in their house, there is a strong concern with keeping order and maintaining the property in immaculate condition. An ordered and clean life is a part of a good life. Their concern with work also is something that they share with their less economically fortunate neighbors among the Einheimischen. And as in the other families, their family and home serves as a center of their lives, rather than as a way station. The Lochers go out from their home to make a living, to acquire the necessary instrumental resources, to experience something of the outside world, but they always return to it as the center of their reality. Their contacts, too, with the outside world are in this same pattern. These contacts, rather than being preoccupying, are secondary to the home. They are restricted and segmentalized. Home is where life comes into focus. Other relationships are peripheral.

DIE ALBRECHT FAMILIE

The Albrecht family, like other families described here, is in transition from a more rural and folk-oriented adaptation to a more urban way of life. The transition for the Albrechts, however, is more abrupt, more dramatic and, therefore, more obvious, than in most. The description to follow focuses upon the more dramatic aspects of this transition.

Falling into conversation with some of the Albrecht boys who are working in the Weinberge[10] on a Saturday afternoon, one finds that they are proud that they own land but that they regard their activity on it as something less than a profession. "We are only helping today. I work in the Bosch factory in Stuttgart. There really isn't any money in the Weinberge these days. We are really only helping. It is just a hobby for us, you might say. There we are all week in the office, you know. It is good to get outside and work, but it is really impossible to make a living that way."

As one goes to their Bauernhaus in Burgbach, one notices the manure pile in its boxlike concrete retainer to the left of the door. It is steaming in the cold of the late afternoon as new additions are pitch-forked out from the stalls behind the thick stone walls. You ring the doorbell and a gray-haired lady leans out a second-

---

[10] Henceforth we will use *Weinberge* rather than "vineyards" or the more cumbersome but more accurate "hilly vineyard plots." The concept of small, distributed, steep vineyard plots is important to keep in mind and will be designated by *Weinberge*. The reader is also reminded that in the context of English sentences only the singular and plural of German nouns are used and no other endings.

story window and indicates that somebody will be right down. One is admitted to the kitchen, which is the center of the family activity. After greeting you, Frau Albrecht resumes peeling potatoes. At the table is Maria, about seventeen, finishing her early dinner and hurrying to get back 'to work. Maria talks very rapidly, "like a machine gun," her teachers always said. It is hard to understand what she is saying but she says, "I can't speak slower, it is not my nature." Wolfing down her food, Maria rises quickly from the table and whisks out of the room, coming back to tease her hair in front of a small mirror hanging from a tack on the kitchen wall. She has on a short skirt and sweater, and wears eye makeup. She bolts toward the door, stops and turns, shakes the hand of the student-visitor, flashes a huge smile and breezes out with, "Auf Wiedersehen." She blows a kiss to her mother, who says automatically, "Sei Brav" (be good). Frau Albrecht shakes her head, "She is really always in a hurry." She continues her tasks for a time, with the visitor sitting quietly. She has already worked all morning and through the early afternoon on the Weinberge. She says she could not go back in the afternoon because of the rain, but "Ich bin zufrieden" (I am satisfied). Asked what she was doing on the land, she explains that she was simply turning the soil with a spade. "But that is hard work," says the visitor. She nods, "One gets used to working until one can no longer live without work. Yes, and here there is not enough work for one day," and she glances around the immaculate room. "My father also had this land. I worked all day yesterday because of the good weather. I am often on the land."

The conversation turned to the children. "Yes, Maria likes to read. So do the boys," said Frau Albrecht. "I don't care to read too much, myself. I read very little. Sometimes when I see Maria reading I tell her she is learning too much. She doesn't need all of that. But she reads anyway. I wanted her to go to housekeeping school (*Hauswirtschaftsschule*) after Grundschule, where she would learn to cook and sew and take care of the house. But she didn't want that at all. She only wants to learn. If I said no, she would always say that she had wanted to learn but that I would not allow it. She might be reproachful against me, and that would not have been good. I don't know how far she will go. Perhaps she will be an accountant's assistant. I don't really know what that means. My mind really doesn't reach that far. I only know that she wants to be that."

The conversation turns to the Flurbereinigung that is destined to take place on the Burgbach Weinberge soon. Frau Albrecht says:

> It is not easy for anyone. There are still many who refuse to give up their land. We have not refused, but it is hard for us too. These Weinberge belonged to my father, and his father before him also had this land. I could never sell it. But if this (Flurbereinigung) takes place, all will be changed.

She went on,

> You know, one never knows what will happen. This land always has value, and money can become worthless at any time. It is truly better if one plants what he uses. Everyone should plant for himself what he is able to. When I am too old to work on this land, I will divide it for my children and they will work it. It is our land. We must keep it, and plant on it. But Heinz doesn't

like to work on the land. Rolf and Adolph still like it for the exercise. We all work together on Saturdays and when there is time. There is always work to be done. Maria? She has her mind elsewhere.

The conversation turns to changes taking place in Burgbach. Frau Albrecht says:

> We are not city people here. We are on the land. Things have changed so much with the newcomers and the Bürgermeister. Once I knew everybody in town, but it is all so grown up now. We are people of the land. It was always important for us to know each other. We helped each other when there was necessity. The Bürgermeister wants to make Burgbach modern. Before he came the streets were not like this [and she pointed out to a well-paved front street]. And in Burgbach, all over town used to be benches under trees where old people could sit and talk. Now there is not a single bench left in Burgbach. He wants to make Burgbach into a city but we are not city people.

She did not appear to be angry as she spoke, but rather talked with an air of resignation.

Herr Albrecht entered the room, having come from tending the livestock. He sat down at the table to have a glass of wine and a piece of Kuchen. The conversation turned again to what would happen to the land when Flurbereinigung did take place. Herr Albrecht says:

> It may make more money for us. It is hard now to get all of this done, traveling around from one piece [of land] to another. We have to duplicate our efforts so much. Even with a tractor, it is not easy to get all of this done. Sometimes we must travel more than it seems we actually work. But all of our land will be in one place after the Flurbereinigung. If we have a bad year and it is not too sunny, it may be that we will suffer. When we have our Weinberge all over, a piece here and a piece there, then no one accident can wipe us out. But times are changing and we must change with them. Some of our methods are old-fashioned. We do not have the hands to make all of that possible. We must learn to use more machinery.

Asked about the interest of his children in land, he said:

> They like to work on the Weinberge as long as it is not a profession. For them it is more interesting to work in the city. They like to work with machinery. The land means something to them, but not as it did for us. For us, there was no life without the land. We could never sell it ourselves. Perhaps they will, when they receive it [by inheritance], but I am not so sure. It is a part of our whole attitude. It comes out sometimes when people grow up. They feel then that they must have some land of their own.

The scene shifts to an evening visit. All of the boys are there as well as Maria and the parents. The boys question the visitor about California, Beverly Hills, Cassius Clay, the draft, the "Black problem," how much girls wear on the California beaches, how long it takes to go from Los Angeles to San Francisco, what the work opportunities are in the United States, how bad the air is in Los Angeles and what is being done about it, what do people really feel about President Nixon. Neither Frau nor Herr Albrecht say very much. Rolf keeps interrupting the conversation with pictures of recent sportscars in which he is very interested and wants to know what the most popular cars are in California. Heinz brings out his new stereo turntable and puts on a recording of Mozart. Adolf wants to talk about a trip that he had taken with a group to Israel. Maria moves from conversation to conversation with curiosity and her machine-gunlike speech. Occasionally, as the visitor addresses questions to Frau or Herr Albrecht, the children will move in quickly as though they feel the stranger would be embarrassed or the parents would find it difficult to talk with them. There is no overt disrespect, but it is as if the children assume that the parents could be of no interest, that their concerns are irrelevant to the experience of the visitor.

Nevertheless, the children and the parents together constitute a unit. They work together on the Weinberge on weekends. The atmosphere in the house is warm and receptive to visitors and family members alike. There is no scorn expressed in the conversations about the older people. It is as Heinz says. "They basically are not a part of the modern world. They clearly do not understand what we are doing. They think only of the land and what it will produce." But in many ways, the children are like the parents. They work hard and save, and think of things that they can acquire or build with their savings, and their ties with the land may not be as shallow as they seem at first. No one can predict what will really happen when the land is theirs. As Rolf says:

> Perhaps if I do not live too far away, I will keep my share. The land has been in our family for a long time, and it is good to get out in the clean air and sunshine and to work with one's body. Sometimes as I am working on the Weinberge I can feel as I think my parents feel, but our lives are not on the land. If I were to move away some place where I could not work on weekends or on off hours, I would probably sell it.

CONCLUSION

It is clear that the variety expressed in the kinds of people in Burgbach is expressed also in the kinds of families in this small community. It may seem that each of these families expresses such a distinctive life style that there are few commonalities, and yet this is not entirely so.

In classroom discussion of family life in Burgbach we began with what might be called the "authoritarian" hypothesis. Much of the literature on Germany, coming out during and after World War II, was centered upon this hypothesis. Nazism and, before that, other political developments in Germany were explained as a consequence of the authoritarian family relationship, or of a national authoritarian personality that was produced in the family, or in the context of other institutions, or both, depending upon the persuasion of the analyst. The father was head of the family and there was little participation in decision making within it.

There has never been very much direct comparative evidence to support a hypothesis that German families were more authoritarian than those of other nationalities. The research by Max Horkheimer in 1936 offered some direct empirical support for a statement that authoritarian patterns were widespread in German families, but no comparative analysis was attempted. The psychiatrist

Dicks (1950a, b) did an interesting analysis of psychological characteristics exhibited by 168 prisoners of war he interviewed extensively. These features, such as an obedience-submission syndrome, and the love of order and hierarchy, could be considered, given certain assumptions, to be an outcome of early experience in an authoritarian family setting. Other research by Bertram Schaffner (1948) reinforces the imagery of authoritarian family patterns. He not only utilized extensive psychological testing, but administered a questionnaire to 2,000 persons representing a wide age and social class range. There have been many other published papers on German character and family life, including one by the author (Spindler 1948), comparing German and American adjustments to military life. Most of these studies were done soon after World War II when objectivity would be difficult.

That there have been authoritarian tendencies in German political and social life would be hard to deny. Whether these tendencies are a function of family life is highly problematic. That there should be some mutual reinforcement between family life and political and social life seems probable. In any event, the authoritarian hypothesis was our starting orientation.

There is little evidence of marked authoritarian patterns in the families with which the student field workers listed in this volume have had contact. It is true that Swabia does not have a reputation as a center of authoritarian values. On the other hand, about half of the families with whom students have had contact were from other parts of Germany including the most northern and the most "Prussian" parts where the authoritarian family type is presumed to be prevalent.

Some families in our selected sample do give some evidence of authoritarian patterns. For example, in the Schmid family there were such patterns, and yet to characterize the family relationships even in this family merely as "authoritarian" would be a distortion of reality. The father's relationship with other members of the family could be described as authoritarian, but he is only one person, playing only certain relatively segmentalized roles in relationship to other members of the family.

There are also subtle "neo-authoritarian" tendencies in other families. The father is often acknowledged as the authority in the outside world while the mother is calmly centered around household and family. This division, however, is clearer among people who have left the land. Among the Weingärtner the woman leaves the house to work side by side with her husband on the land and takes an important responsibility within the economic as well as domestic side of the household. There is a strong egalitarianism in this relationship.

It may seem that a form of authoritarianism is operating in the exacting and constant supervision of the children's activities by parents. Perhaps the children feel this to be the case. Nevertheless, this relationship does not take classical authoritarian forms. The father does not give short, unexplained orders to other members of the family. Rather, the relationship is one of closeness and of intense interaction.

What is much more obvious than authoritarianism is the *centripetal* character of family life. The home is a center of activity rather than a launching pad for other places and other activities, as the American middle class family and home so often are. People in Burgbach work in order to maintain the home, and having maintained it, use it as the focus and center of their lives. Children stay with the family longer than is the case in the American household, and seem to return to it for longer visits and more often after they have grown up and have left home. The family also tends toward a certain kind of isolation. The circle of relationships is restricted to relatives and close friends, and frequently only to relatives. There is relatively low interest in or involvement with outside affairs in the immediate community, although more distant affairs may be a matter of great curiosity. Security, the inner family life, the feeling of *Gemütlichkeit* (geniality) is most important. These tendencies seem to run clearly through all of the families described and in the larger sample from which these were selected.

Perhaps it is the relative isolation, the segmentalization of relationships, the family-centeredness, that is more relevant to certain events in Germany than the authoritarian character and the presumed authoritarian family standing behind it. As long as one's family life is all right, there may be little concern with what happens outside. Social and political movements can get out of hand in such an environment. Morality applies first to the inner circle. One is not responsible for what happens outside. To be left alone to work and live, to enjoy life within the family and home, these are the primary values, not what happens in the outside world.[11]

There are some other tendencies held in common by these Burgbach families: the careful use of space, of which there is not much; the frugality about expenditures; the emphasis placed upon work, cleanliness, and respectability. These fundamental values appear in one form or another in all the families described. Their quality is somewhat different for the Schwaben than for the others, but there is a sharing that seems to supercede the specific cultural and life style differences. Even in the one family described in which there is some ostentatious display of material possessions, and material competition with the neighbors, there is no real waste, and family-centeredness is a prime value.

Perhaps it is the commonalities that help make possible the apparent assimilation of potentially dissident elements, representing all the major social aggregates, into a formerly homogeneous community. Despite differences, there are many ways in which the people in the families are like each other. At the same time, perhaps the social system works effectively with its potentially dissident elements because each family is inward-oriented and self-sufficient. People find their major satisfaction within the family. Public roles and public conflicts can be segmentalized and governed by formal conventions that preserve the appearance of harmony whether it is actually present or not. Perhaps it is for this reason that formal etiquette and ritual are important in social life in the Remstal, as they are elsewhere in Germany. They make possible interaction between people whose real lives take place at home and who are acting out roles self-consciously in public.

That there are significant differences between families and individuals, as well as commonalities, is obvious. Not only are newcomers different from natives, not

[11] Ralf Dahrendorf provides a somewhat similar analysis in his *Society and Democracy* (1967), particularly in Chapters 19 and 20. I had not read this book before writing this case study.

only are the rich different from the people who must be careful about expenditures (though there are few really very poor people in the area), but there are even greater differences between the younger generation moving away from the land and the older generation tied to it. It does seem, however, that the value placed upon the land, upon work and frugality, upon the careful appraisal of all possibilities, and the high valuation of family life are common threads connecting the past with the present, and all of the Einheimischen to each other. The newcomers share with the rest the value put upon family life, work, and frugality.

4 / Forces for cultural continuity

INTRODUCTION

Anthropologists have devoted considerable time and energy to the problem of how cultures change. It is also important to try to understand why cultures persist, especially when changing conditions of existence seem to call for trans-formative adaptation. It is clear that all cultures are constantly changing, though at varying rates, but that these changes take place within a framework of meaning and material adaptation accumulated from the past. In the next chapter, we will deal with forces for change in Burgbach and their consequences. In this chapter we will analyze some significant forces supporting cultural persistence and continuity.

The forces for persistence are grouped in four categories in the analysis to follow. They are: reaffirmation of identity; self-verifying beliefs; ecological "lock-in"; and ritualization. We will illustrate each with specific examples. It should be clear, however, that we are not merely concerned with specific instances of the persistence of cultural forms or the continuity of contemporary behavior with the traditional culture. We attempt in this chapter to expose some generalizable forces for cultural persistence and continuity that underlie the specific forms of these processes. These forces are present in varying degrees in all of the specific cases of cultural persistence that will be discussed. Each case, however, has been selected as a particularly good example of one of these forces. Reaffirmation of identity will be illustrated by the *Kirbefest*, a four-day celebration that is held every autumn; self-verifying beliefs by *Volksheilkunde*, the folk medicine that is very widespread in Germany; and ecological "lock-in" by analysis of certain patterns of land use. Ritualization, it will be seen, is a force for cultural persistence that operates in all these situations. What we mean by ritualization can only be understood fully in context, but it will be introduced at an abstract level now. It will appear again at various points in the analysis to follow.

RITUALIZATION

Ritualization permeates virtually all of human behavior. It is most obvious in formal rituals, as in a traditional wedding ceremony, a church service, a funeral, a

51

The Weingärtner must be highly skilled at a wide variety of tasks, including pruning the vines so as to encourage new growth. (Courtesy Rick Hanson.)

confirmation, or on ceremonial state occasions. We are not mainly concerned with these forms of rituals, however. Nor are we particularly concerned with another class of easily recognized ritual behaviors, such as social amenities, dress, grooming, the habitual sequence involved in getting up in the morning, going to bed at night, or reading the newspaper. Most rituals of this kind are recognized by people as such.

We are more concerned with behaviors that are not so easily recognized as rituals, and may not be thought of as rituals at all, even by social scientists. And we are not as interested in rituals as we are in the process of ritualization. Ritualization occurs in virtually every behavioral context. Traditional usages are often, perhaps always, ritualized, though tradition and ritual are, as we use these concepts, not identical.

Ritualization, as we think of it, occurs whenever the means to an end become habitualized and provide satisfactions only tangentially or not at all related to the original goal. These ritualized means tend to persist, sometimes for centuries, beyond the original ends that were functional in a given context now changed. A minor and rather obvious example is provided by the buttons on the sleeves of men's coats and jackets. Once functional as fasteners for gauntleted gloves worn by knights, they are now ritualized forms that have no relationship to the original end. They provide esthetic satisfaction. They provide social security for they are now a part of being well dressed. Similar processes have occurred in every complex of custom. That there are different kinds of rituals, perhaps several types of ritualization processes, seems clear, but they have common features.

If not clearly destructive to the survival of a community, or to an individual, rituals may go on endlessly, since they provide satisfactions and are not usually subject to objective evaluation concerning their efficacy as instrumental, goal-directed behaviors. They do have esthetic and security-giving functions which may become very important. As long as conditions do not change so that their substitute (ritualized) functions become destructive, there is no reason why they should be eliminated. In fact, their elimination will usually be resisted by the people whose rituals they are, and attempts to eliminate them may do damage. They are often merely harmless and in fact gratifying flourishes, as in the case of the buttons. They are often primary sources of security, as in religion. In certain economic, political, and educational contexts, however, ritualization may become profoundly dysfunctional, for it is usually not recognized for what it is, and is defended as though it were the end, the goal, of the action. Rituals become fixed in the perceptual and motivational patterns of participants, because they provide esthetic satisfaction, predictability, and security. Alternative ways of proceeding to the original goal cannot be recognized, or if recognized, cannot be acted upon.

Ritualization is a significant process in the stabilization of cultural forms and therefore in what is usually referred to as "tradition." It occurs in the context of economic behavior, where rationalized behavior has high utility, as well as in areas of life where ritualized behavior would seem more probable such as religion and in social interaction. Much of the current planned program development in German agriculture, an important area of economic behavior, is directed at "rationalizing" agricultural practice. Rationalization, in this context, means to organize the means of production with the greatest possible efficiency in relationship to the desired end product. Rationalization is implemented to eliminate nonrational practices which interfere with this relationship. Many such practices are the result of ritualization. The ritualization of certain aspects of economic behavior will be discussed under ecological "lock-in." An important example of rationalization will be discussed in Chapter 5.

We now turn to a discussion of the Kirbefest. The Kirbefest is a traditional complex of behaviors and symbols composed largely of ritualized elements drawn from the past. It functions in today's context as a reaffirmation of the identity of Burgbach, an identity that is becoming irrelevant in the urbanizing Remstal.

REAFFIRMATION OF IDENTITY AND THE KIRBEFEST

Reaffirmation of identity occurs whenever there is a public demonstration of relatedness to the traditions or legends of the past, or to community symbols. Burgbach, as we have seen, has several claims to a significant identity in the history of the Remstal. These claims are presented and defended in various publications supported by the community. The Heimatbuch from which we drew in Chapter 1 is an example. A leaflet handed to visitors titled *Burgbach : Wein und Ausflugsort* (wine and excursion village) is another. This leaflet is illustrated with beautiful pictures of Burgbach in full color including the altar in the Stifts-kirche, the roses along the brook until recently running through the center of town (it is now canalized and covered over with pavement), and an aerial view of the part of the valley in which Burgbach lies. It also provides a brief excerpt from the legendary history of Burgbach, emphasizing as does the Heimatbuch the fact that Burgbach is the cradle, on the maternal side, of the lords of Württemberg. This brochure also provides an idealized statement of the development of Burgbach since the war. The great increase of population, industry, building, and the modernization and improvement of all existing facilities is stressed. The brochure ends with a statement that the core of the community is the old and well-beloved landmarks and that the community remains true to its historical traditions. Burgbach, it states, is today at the same time a Weinort and an *Industriegemeinde* (industrial community).

The reaffirmation of Burgbach identity, however, goes well beyond the publication and distribution of the Heimatbuch and the brochure for visitors. The artistic and very modernisticly cast concrete mural depicting the events of the peasant revolution (der Arme Konrad) in the new Rathaus is a reaffirmation. And there are several communitywide ceremonial events that are reaffirmative. The most important of these ceremonial events is the Kirbefest. This four-day ritual celebration takes place each October. As will be seen, it is an intermingling of elements drawn from the harvest festival, days of both pagan and Christian worship, market day, and from rites of passage for young boys and girls. It will be described as a significant example of a reaffirmation of identity that supports cultural persistence, as do all such reaffirmations.

The Kirbefest

The Burgbach Kirbefest is traditionally held during the last week of October from Thursday through Sunday. The sequence of events within this four-day period varies from year to year, as do the scope and kinds of activity connected with them. Certain features, however, are more or less consistently represented and they will be described.

The early Christian missionaries to the "heathens" in southern Germany during the first centuries of the Christian expansion did not impose the whole structure of this belief on their clients. They substituted a Saints' Day for the day of worship of "Tor," "Tonner," or "Donner." This became a general day of praise for the saints and a part of the evolving Burgbach Kirbe very early in the history of the community. The term "Kirbe" is a contraction of "Kirchweih," or of "Kirichwehi," in Old High German, meaning a dedication to the consecration of the saints of the early Catholic Church in Germany. The sacred elements, however, have almost disappeared in the present celebration and appear as only a vestige in the extra church services offered and attended by some.

More important in the present sequence of ceremonial observances is the Market Day. Burgbach early in its history became an important market town. It was strategically located in the valley, and since Roman times it had been a substantial population cluster. We do not know when Market Day as a part of the fall festival actually began, but we do know that in 1280 Count Ulrich, possessor of the castle on the Kappelberg overlooking Burgbach, had already granted the right of market to the village. Since that time this right has been denied and then regranted several times. In 1797 a *"Marktordnung"* was written by a Judge Bilfinger, proclaiming the reestablishment of the "twice prevented rightful horse, cattle, shopkeeper, and flax market." The document is written in the archaic script of the eighteenth century. Though it appeared much later than the early beginnings of the Kirbe, the ordinances contained within it provide a description of what had been the procedure for some time prior to 1797 and therefore representative of its traditional form.

The preparation for the market began five days ahead of the last Thursday of the month. The Town Crier announced the market on the Saturday previous to it and everyone was directed to keep the area around his or her house clean and a special Market Director was appointed to see that lumber, rocks, dung, and other obtrusive trash was carried away. Precautions were taken to see that the fire wagon was immediately available and that there was a large tub of water in front of every door since the danger of fire during Market Day was great.

The Market Director was also responsible for seeing to it that the itinerant shopkeepers who put up their stands on Market Day did so properly and that they gave the people a fair deal. He was aided in the keeping of order by a corps of sixteen men, including a corporal, a drummer, and a piper from the People's Militia.

At 9 o'clock on Thursday morning the militia paraded through the streets with the drum and fife going strong, the rough board stands were made ready and the wares displayed. People had gathered by horse, foot, and wagon from all over the Remstal to begin a merry day of haggling, bargaining, drinking, singing, and occasional brawling.

Each trader was assigned a certain place for his stand. All of one street directly adjacent to the present market place was assigned to shoemakers, saddlers, and tanners, while another was assigned to lockmakers, nail, copper, and metal smiths. In the upper area of the market place were rope makers, bookbinders, bottle makers, and tinsmiths. The stocking, cloth, tub makers, and knitters were in the lower part of the market area in front of one of the present *Gasthäuser*.[1] In the center of the area were wooden wares such as ladders, furniture, and small household objects, and on the outskirts of the market were the pig, cow, horse, and sheep stalls as well as farm equipment. A committee consisting of a magistrate, the Market Director, and a member of the militia checked all measuring instruments used by traders and confiscated earnings from anyone who was caught cheating.

Today the market elements are still maintained, though as a vestige of their traditional form. Thursday is still a market day during the Kirbe festival and the shopkeepers still put up stands along the streets as they did centuries ago. But they are not divided according to trade and ware. Cheap jewelry, sweaters, underwear, household objects, shoes, socks, mittens, pots and pans, antiques, notions of various kinds, all can be bought at reduced prices. The people seem to enjoy the

---

[1] *Gasthäuser* are like taverns or pubs but usually have facilities for overnight guests and serve food.

open market and examine the goods, buy occasionally, and particularly if the weather is bad, as it is frequently is, turn into a Gasthaus for a friendly glass of wine or beer. The attendance at the Market Day is surprisingly high, given its economically irrelevant and generally nonfunctional character, and a substantial crowd mills around the stands happily for several hours.

The Kirbe "*Mädle* und *Buble*," boys and girls of seventeen to nineteen, are the symbolic leaders and practical helpers during the Kirbefest. The tradition apparently began during the days when nineteen-year-old boys were required to leave home to serve in the army and the village recognized their last days at home by honoring them during the Kirbe. For the girls, there is something of the "coming-out party" atmosphere. The tradition persists, though the original functions are more or less irrelevant today.

Special costumes are chosen by the group and then made by mother-daughter teams. In one recent festival the girls wore blue and white checked cotton dresses with small vests and scooped necks. They were only faintly "peasant-looking" and could be worn again, even in Stuttgart. Around their necks the girls wore a white and red flowered scarf. The boys wore white shirts, black pants, and a bright red vest decorated with brass buttons. A white and red scarf similar to that worn by the girls was tied around their necks with a match box for a tie clasp.

This group of boys and girls is together much of the time during the four days of the fest, particularly during the Friday and Saturday night dances. The main duty of the group is "Lustig zu sein" (to be gay), as these young people are technically the hosts and hostesses of the Kirbe.

During the four days of the fest a large pear-shaped cluster of grapes (*Kirbetraube*) weighing about 50 pounds and approximately 4 feet long by 3 feet wide, at its widest point, is hung on the Marktstrasse outside of one of the popular Gasthäuser. It is the symbol of the Burgbach Kirbe and is made from great bunches of purple grapes tied to hooks on a wire frame. The Kirbe youth must "steal" the grapes, and make and hang the Kirbetraube while singing the Kirbe song.

> *Einmal im Jahr, soll Burgbacher Kirbe sein,*
> *Einmal im Jahr, da wollen wir alle im Remstal sein,*
> *Einmal im Jahr, da wollen wir alle fröhlich sein,*
> *Wir trinken den Wein und küssen die Mädle,*
> *Und wer noch dumm ist wird gescheit,*
> *Darum schenket ihn ein,*
> *den Burgbacher Wein.*

(Once a year there should a Burgbach Kirbe be,
Once a year, then want we all to be in Remstal,
Once each year, we want all of us there to be happy,
We drink the wine, and kiss the girls,
And who is still dumb will become smart,
So go ahead and pour it in,
The Burgbach wine.)

On Friday morning the Kirbe Mädle and Buble decorate the townhall with greens, and each girl bakes a few Kuchen. The day's activities are highlighted with a dance for which the young people act as hosts and hostesses. On Saturday the main event is also the dance that night, but various observances occur during the day and there is a great deal of moving about from Gasthaus to Gasthaus and from one private home to another for wine and Kuchen. For the Kirbe Mädle and Buble the big event during the day is a ride on a float pulled by a tractor through neighboring villages. There is much laughing, shouting, and loud singing, and much stopping at people's houses and at an occasional Gasthaus for wine. The group proceeds through the streets with a great deal of racket made by horns and by wooden noisemakers which are used ordinarily to scare birds away from the grapes in the fall. The dance that night is a continuation of the general merriment and is attended by people of all ages.

On Sunday after church services, the crowd gathers around the Kirbetraube and a Kirbe Bubele reads a poem of thanks for a bountiful harvest. Usually about one o'clock the big parade begins led by a band composed mostly of members of the Musikverein (musical club), followed by two persons dressed as Luitgart von Burgbach and her husband, representing the Württemberg royal line, and in turn followed by their train. After them come townspeople dressed in traditional costumes, many of them representing the main personages of the Rebellion of the Arme Konrad. Then come elders in the cloaks of various traditional religious orders, followed by members of the sports clubs dressed as warriors of the Thirty Years War. Then the Kirbe Buble and Mädle in their costumes come swinging and singing down the street, followed finally by decorated floats representing stores and business establishments in Burgbach or the immediate vicinity.

Interpretation

The elements and patterns that make up the present-day Kirbe festival are largely derived out of Burgbach's past through a process of ritualization. They have become a part of the ceremonial sequence and though once functional, as symbols of significant beliefs or activities, have now become attenuated in terms of their original meaning. Nevertheless, these elements persist for they have a place in the ceremonial sequence; they have become ritualized and produce satisfactions unrelated to their original meanings or functions. They have also acquired meaning as an observance of Burgbach unity and identity.

The Saints' Day was long ago substituted for a day of "pagan" worship. Only vestiges of religious observance are retained in the present Kirbefest, however, for the religious significance of the festival is the least meaningful in the modern context. Religious elements were displaced early by secular patterns in the evolution of behavior in the festival. In contrast, the rites of passage for the young boys and girls about to enter adulthood, implied by their participation as hosts and hostesses in the ceremonies and particularly in the dances, survive relatively intact. Though the association with the military service of the boys and the "coming-out party" for the girls is less meaningful now, a deeper meaning may be found in the association with the symbols of the harvest and their implications of fertility. The community has an opportunity to reassure itself of its continuity into the future with the symbolic recognition of a new generation of young people in each Kirbe festival and an implicit recognition of their fertility in the celebration of the harvest. The trip of the youngsters on their float to the nearby villages is an announcement of this renewed continuity (and fertility) to what were traditionally competitors, and not always friendly ones, with Burgbach.[2]

The Market Day was once of considerable economic significance. Burgbach had no shops when Judge Bilfinger described Market Day in 1797 and it had very few even as late as 1960. The Market Day served as an economic stimulant, distributed necessary goods as well as luxuries and provided an opportunity for social intercourse. All of these functions were important in the Remstal of bygone days. The Market Day persists as a remnant of its past glory but it is still a significant element in the Kirbe festival. It is a clear example of ritualization. The Market Day cannot serve its original purpose in contemporary Burgbach. It produces satisfaction, however, for reasons quite unrelated to its original purpose. It serves no necessary or even useful economic function, yet people come and mill about the stalls that for the most part exhibit wares which they do not need.

The harvest elements, represented most obviously by the Kirbetraube and the poem of thanks for the harvest, but indirectly represented by the abundance of food and drink at the various gatherings of the festival, are probably elements of very long standing. The more explicit fertility elements probably once present have been lost or are only metaphorically present, but the harvest itself, and particularly the Kirbetraube, is a symbol of fertility. These rituals and symbols may stretch back far into the history and even prehistory of the Remstal.

Whatever the past significance of the various elements now patterned together into a loosely integrated whole, the Kirbefest functions to reaffirm a village identity. Among participants interviewed about their interpretation of the Kirbefest, it was often explicit that indeed this was a "Heimatfest," a celebration designed to draw people closer to the village. The dances, the various skits that lampooned village members or events, the costumes, and the Kirbetraube itself are all seen as parts of a heimat-rooted complex. It is also seen as an opportunity for visits with friends, for showing the inhabitants' general concern with town events, and for having a good time. As one lady said, "Naturally we are happy to have our own Kirbe. We can have a good time and, at the same time, show respect for our traditions." Or as one Weingärtner said, "For me, and all of us, our Kirbe is the real Fest of our village."

The Kirbe festival also persists not merely as a ritualized reaffirmation of historical identity, but because cultural adaptations of broader dimensions still persist of which it is an expression. The Kirbetraube has a direct material significance. There is a harvest, and a very significant one, of wine grapes in the fall. The wine produced from those grapes is an important factor in the economy of the region. The Kirbetraube is a symbolic reaffirmation of that significance. Further, the Kirbefest is made more meaningful because Burgbach is still a Weinort, still has Bauernhäuser, much of its population still speaks Schwäbisch, and for these reasons it has pride in its rootedness in the past. That this relationship is circular is obvious. There is circularity in the relationship between symbol,

[2] The trip to other villages was not included in 1971 due to traffic and "other considerations." It is probable that the competition with other communities has become irrelevant with increasing urbanization.

action, and function in all ceremonial contexts. The Kirbefest persists because Burgbach persists in some degree as a Weinort, and vice versa. It is an event in which people find meaning and pleasure. The Kirbefest persists because it is a reaffirmation of the identity of Burgbach and the relationship of this identity to the past. Burgbach continues to exist as an identifiable community partly because of this reaffirmation, at the same time providing the basis for the ceremonial observance of its continued existence.

It would be misleading to end the description and analysis of the Kirbefest without mentioning the fact that not all of the Burgbacher are equally enthusiastic about it. A number of the *Zugezogenen*[3] (newcomers) do not even bother to attend the celebration and regard the noise and confusion in the streets as a considerable nuisance. An increasing number of young people also regard the Kirbefest as an anachronism, and a few of the more radical youth regard it as an unacceptable form of establishmentarianism and something to be destroyed. As of 1971, however, the Kirbefest was held with most of the described elements represented.

We now turn to another category of forces supporting cultural continuity—self-verifying beliefs—using Volksheilkunde as an example.

SELF-VERIFYING BELIEFS

Self-verifying beliefs are fundamental to the continuation of all cultural systems. The ideational dimensions of a culture may be considered to be a complex patterning of such beliefs. As long as these beliefs do not violate conditions imposed by material reality so drastically as to threaten the survival of the community, beliefs about the nature of reality which are quite in error will continue to flourish indefinitely.

For example, water witching and discovery of precious metals using water-witching techniques, widespread in North America as well as Europe, apparently work on this basis. The procedure involves walking about with a forked willow stick (or a coathanger, chain, coin in a glass of water, etc.) over areas where the well or excavation should be located and where the "witch" has usually decided there should be water or metals, until involuntary movements in the muscles of the hands and arms of the witch cause the "instrument" to dip, swing, or move in some way. There is no objective evidence to date to indicate that water witching works as well as scientifically controlled knowledge about ground water or minerals. However, the technique "works" frequently enough, particularly in the case of witching for water, given the existence of ground water at some depth in most areas of the world, to confirm it from the nonscientific point of view.[4] In the United States as well as in Germany, most wells are probably "witched" before

3 This term will be used henceforth since it is more accurate than "newcomers" or immigrants. Please see glossary.
4 It should be noted that even if it were proven that under certain conditions water witching "really" works, the self-verifying principle would still hold good, for no empirically controlled evidence had been used to validate the efficacy of the ritual during the centuries it has been applied.

they are drilled or dug. Since the general area in which the well is to be located has already been selected for other reasons, including surface indications, based on local experience, of probable ground water, the witching ritual serves to confirm the choice and specify the exact location of the well, thus reducing anxiety over the decision about where to dig or drill. Failures in the location of water or detection of precious metals are often taken as confirming evidence. A metal knife, for example, in the pocket of the "witch" may short-circuit the "electromagnetic waves" believed by some to be the basis for the apparent action of the detecting implement (willow stick or whatever). The technique has also been used to identify criminals and find lost objects (Vogt and Hyman 1959).

Another example can be provided by any religion. Religious systems operate as self-verifying patterns of belief about the nature of unseen forces, places, beings, man's fate, and man himself. Rituals and self-verifying beliefs intergrade and reinforce each other in all aspects of culturally influenced behavior. Many beliefs are, in fact, a product of the ritualization process. Rituals and self-verifying beliefs are particularly characteristic of religions, since controlled verification of beliefs and the efficacy of ritualized behavior is particularly difficult in this area. One's own religion, or faith, becomes "true" while someone else's becomes "superstition" or "magical thinking." The same logic is applicable to any other aspect of culture where controlled, objective evidence and canons of evidence are not available, or if available, are not used.

Volksheilkunde

Cultural definitions of disease, its detection and cure, constitute a particularly fertile area for the proliferation and maintenance of self-verifying beliefs, for health and illness are intimately linked with personal and communal survival, and are areas of belief and behavior where anxiety is omnipresent. It is this area which we will now consider. Volksheilkunde—"folk healing"—is present in some form in most homes in Burgbach. Some of Volksheilkunde is physiologically as well as psychologically effective. Volksheilkunde beliefs are, however, self-verifying without external, controlled evidence, simply because most people with minor, and many with major, diseases or hurts recover with or without treatment. Volksheilkunde also has contributed to the maintenance of other cultural subsystems, as do all self-verifying beliefs and ritualized behaviors. Volksheilkunde is imbedded in the family, which, as we have seen, is a particularly significant social unit in Burgbach, as elsewhere in Germany.

Various forms of Volksheilkunde are represented not only at the informal level of ordinary household remedies passed on from parent to child, but also in remedies sold in *Drogerien* (stores resembling drugstores but not selling prescriptions) as well as in remedies for disease syndromes described in textbooks approved by the State Ministry of Education for use in the Grundschule. There is a very substantial literature on Volksheilkunde in its various forms that ranges all the way from technical, seemingly scientific treatises, to a useful book to have around the house called *Unser Hausfreund* (Roff 1956).

It is difficult for Americans to understand Volksheilkunde. Many Americans use home remedies and nearly all use aspirin or something similar for almost every conceivable psychological or physiological complaint. Volksheilkunde in its most complete form, however, goes far beyond this. It is a set of attitudes and beliefs that is supported not only by folk in the most remote village, but also to some extent by professional medical personnel. Volksheilkunde is not merely a survival from the past, although it contains many elements from the past. It is a living pattern. It contains within its total range not only concepts and behaviors that are probably medically effective, but also many that seem to be heavily ritualized. These are not mutually exclusive categories, for ritual behaviors often have decisive psychosomatic effects. The borderline between what is pragmatically valid and what is magical belief or ritualized behavior, particularly in medical practice, is extremely difficult to ascertain. We can define this shadowy area better by describing a sample of Volksheilkunde beliefs and remedies. We will consider common home remedies, therapeutic bathing, and Heilkräuter-tee (healing tea).

Common Home Remedies

Among twenty-five women interviewed in Burgbach representing the major life styles and social aggregates described in the last chapter, the following remedies were commonly used at home.

Toothache: hold a warm clay-filled sack on the stricken area; bite on cloves; chew hard black bread; use hot compresses; use schnapps-saturated cotton wads; put clove oil on the sore spot; put clove oil on a cotton wad stuffed into the cavity.

Infection and fever: drink a lot of water and other liquids; drink camomile and peppermint teas; drink Lindenblüten tea; wrap the calves of the leg or the entire upper part of the body with compresses soaked in a water-and-vinegar solution; wrap infected areas with compresses of sour milk or pig lard.

Headaches: wrap the head with a compress soaked with water, vinegar, and milk; drink various teas; take a cool foot bath.

Sneezing and coughing: drink honey and cognac mixed together with hot water and lemon; wear a flannel cloth with camphor on the chest; use a vaporizer to which vinegar has been added; inhale camomile-tea steam and drink hot camomile tea; rub oil and fat compresses on the chest; drink onion juice with brown sugar, or drink radish juice with brown sugar; take a steam bath with the addition of camomile tea or eucalyptus oil; drink hot malt wine; drink lemon juice; use a sweat cure.

Insomnia: drink Baldrian tea; eat onions which have been boiled in milk immediately before retiring; drink a mixture of cold milk and honey; place the bed with the feet toward the south and the head toward the north; sleep with the head higher than the feet.

Stomach aches, cramps, and heartburn: drink various cognacs and schnapps; eat zwieback; drink Baldrian and bloodroot teas; drink peppermint tea and put warm cloths on the stomach.

Constipation: eat sour milk or cottage cheese; eat apples and drink apple juice; chew tobacco and swallow the juice; sit in a tub of warm water; use suppositories, particularly in the form of a small splinter of soap; drink honey and water on an empty stomach; eat raw sauerkraut; use any one of a number of medicinal herb teas (*Kräuterteen*).

Burns: use salad oils as a dressing; use butter or codliver oil and bind with muslin; make a paste of vegetable oil and potato meal; cover with the white of a fresh egg; use a compress soaked with one of several teas.

Diarrhea: eat zwieback and drink cold red wine; fast and then drink black teas and zwieback; chew and swallow charcoal; eat oatmeal; drink hot chocolate cooked with water instead of milk; drink a raw egg mixed with cognac; drink a number of herbs mixed together and steeped, including Kamillenblüten and Anis.

Worms: eat garlic and onions or raw carrots; take honey, use an enema of salt and soap water; drink mineral water with pumpkin or gourd seeds; drink hot milk; use one of several teas recommended for worms.

It is quite impossible to separate out precisely what is "sound" medical practice and what is ritualized or magical practice in these remedies. There is a mixture of physiologically relevant and irrelevant. For our purposes it is not important that this separation be made. Irrespective of their medical efficacy or lack of it, these remedies will be used without objective evidence of their efficacy. They are self-sustaining beliefs as applied by the people who use them. They all provide something for the members of the household to do for someone who is stricken with minor illness or hurts. The probability that the patient will recover, regardless of what is done, is high. Therefore almost any practice that is not downright harmful is validated. Even harmful practices, to the extent that they do not result in the death of the patient, may be validated by eventual recovery, temporary remission of symptoms or partial recovery.

We do not mean to imply that in the homes where these remedies are used professional medical help is not called for or employed. Nearly all German families are covered by health insurance programs, and in a community like Burgbach medical help is relatively easily available. The women interviewed pointed out that the conditions treated were all minor. They said that when a serious condition developed, medical help is always used. They pointed out further that there was no necessary contradiction between the use of professional medical help and the use of home remedies of this type.

Therapeutic Bathing

Therapeutic bathing is widely used in Germany both in standard medical practice and in home treatment of minor illnesses or chronic, nonacute conditions not requiring hospitalization. It is also featured in many curing spas scattered throughout the Black Forest and other vacation areas.

Among the twenty-five Burgbach women interviewed on health practices as well as thirty other households in which relevant inquiries were made in the context of other studies, therapeutic bathing in some form was used, even if it meant no more than taking a hot bath with the addition of one of several aromatic solutions that are readily available on the market. Some baths that appeared to be heavily ritualized are used rather infrequently but are known by nearly all the persons interviewed.

In general, therapeutic bathing is regarded as an aid to nature in the disposal of body poisons, as a means of strengthening nerves, arousing appetite, improving digestion, and enlivening circulation and metabolism. The baths are of several types.

Sitzbad: a simple tub bath (in which one sits) which achieves maximum results with the coldest possible water.
Mud bath: the same as Sitzbad but with approximately one kilogram (2.2 lbs) of silt mixed in with the water.

The Luftlichtbad: the body is sprinkled with water and then the bather runs around naked breathing deeply.

The Reibebad: the bather sits on a small bench in the tub, dips a towel into cold water and vigorously rubs the body from the pit of the stomach down. The feet must be kept dry.

Dampfbad: steam from boiling hay blossoms, oats, straw, or zinnia is directed upon the afflicted part of the body and the part is covered with a saturated cloth to hinder evaporation.

Bettdampfbad: the naked patient is wrapped in a sheet which has been immersed in lukewarm water. He or she is covered with wool blankets, and hot water bottles are placed on the armpits and feet. After sweating for one or two hours the patient is washed with cool water.

Ganzwaschung: one begins by washing the right foot and then the left foot, continuing on up to the hips on the foresides of the legs, followed by the backsides. After this, the upper body is washed starting with the right arm and followed by the left arm and continuing to the left breast, downwards to the stomach, then up the right side to the breast, followed in turn by the side parts of the body, and finally the back. Some authorities recommend no drying with towels.

Many additives to the various warm and cold baths may be used. Hay flowers are believed to stimulate the skin and to relieve arthritis, rheumatism, and lung congestion. When added to bath water spruce needles, or one of the many commercial preparations of similar character, through their aroma, it is believed, work to calm the nervous system and stimulate blood circulation and metabolism. Oak bark is useful as an additive for various skin diseases, hemorrhoids, and tuberculosis of the lymph glands. Camomile is added to the bath to treat colds with fever, eczema, wounds, hemorrhoids, blisters, and various infections and abdominal complaints. Bran makes the skin soft when added to bath water and is used for skin diseases, eczema, and psoriasis. Mustard is one of the strongest stimulants and is used for grippe, bronchitis, lung inflammation, headache, and congestion of any kind. Very often these substances are taken in the context of a *Wechselbad*. This kind of bath begins with a few minutes of warm to fairly hot water and ends with several seconds in cold water. This is believed to have a beneficial and stimulating effect on circulation.

The same general remarks can be made about therapeutic bathing as can be made about home remedies. It is clear that variation in the temperature of bath water, including sweating, and probably even the vapors from the various herbs added to the bath water have physiological effects which may, indeed, be beneficial in the treatment of certain conditions and for certain patients. They may also, it is assumed, be harmful in the treatment of certain conditions. For persons not seriously debilitated by illness, they probably induce a general feeling of well being. In any event, they are again something that one can do about one's condition or for someone else in the family.

All of the baths, even those that do have definite beneficial physiological effect, involve ritual elements which in themselves create psychoemotional states which may be further effective in producing satisfactions only tangentially or not at all related to curing specific ailments. The highly ritualized baths, such as the complex Ganzwaschung, must produce these benefits entirely through the ritual process itself.

Heilkräuter-tee

Heilkräuter-tee (tea from medicinal herbs) is widely used in Germany on a very casual basis for the treatment of practically any minor condition and as an aid to recovery from more serious ones. Nearly every Drogerie in the Remstal area sells a wide variety of such teas. *Apotheken*[5] sell medicinal herbs as teas as well as prescription and pharmaceutical products, including aspirin and other common household drugs that do not require professional supervision for their use in the United States. There are few households which do not use medicinal herb teas. Most people simply assume that they are beneficial and useful, though people in the highest educational levels tend to be more skeptical about any home remedies, therapeutic baths, or herbal teas. The reading books of the third and fourth grade in the Grundschule, however, contain several pages describing and listing specific herbal teas and their presumed effect. Many students reported that they were offered teas by the families they were observing whenever they had a headache or if they professed to be coming down with a cold, or suffering with a mild stomach disorder, or from general malaise.

There are at least eighty domestic medicinal herbs which can be used alone or mixed to form *Komplex Kräuter* (mixtures of medicinal herbs). The six listed below are the most commonly used, according to local *Drogisten*.

Anis (anis seed) stimulates action of digestive organs, brings relief from asthma, and is good for colic in children.
Fenchel (fennel) is good for coughs and asthma, strengthens nerves in the stomach and intestines, and is good as an eye wash and to strengthen the optic nerve.
Kamille (camomile) helps relieve almost any form of stomach pains, spasms, or cramps, especially when mixed with peppermint tea; calms nerves, and when dissolved in bath water helps arrest inflammation or reduce swelling; also used as a hair dressing and bleaching and darkening hair.
Linde (lime tree blossom) is good for colds, stomach cramps, and in general for soothing, tranquilizing effects, and, in solution, useful as a skin cleanser.
Minze (mint or peppermint) is especially good for the stimulation of the kidneys, helps weak hearts, soothes the restless and worried, and should be taken every day.
Salbei (sage) strengthens stomach and intestinal walls, helps remove blockages in the liver and gall passages, is good as a gargle against throat irritation, and helps reduce "night-sweating."

There are also a very large number of commercially prepared tea complexes made up of mixes of several of the eighty common domestic herbs used for teas and labeled according to the body part or organ or the type of disease for which they are believed effective. Some of these sold most frequently in local Remstal Drogerien are listed below.

Abführ-Tee: helps clean intestines, ridding them of digestive wastes and preventing constipation, also recommended for hemorrhoids.
8-Blüten-Tee (*Schlaf-und-Nerven-Tee*): this eight blossom sleep-and-nerve tea regulates sleep and calms and strengthens the nerves.

---

[5] It should be clear that there is no precise equivalent to the American drugstore in Germany. The Drogerie comes closest because everything from toothpaste to film may be sold in them, but only Apotheken have prescription counters—and many medicines, such as aspirin, require prescriptions.

Blutkreislauf-Tee: this tea for improving circulation of the blood is believed to be good for arteriosclerosis and high blood pressure; it cleans and freshens the blood and should be a daily drink for the middle-aged and aged.

Blutreinigungs-Tee: this blood-cleansing and disinfecting tea should be taken every year in the spring and fall. The "herbal hormones" in the tea are believed to effect the removal of waste materials that occur as a result of chemical changes in the body and also to relieve general tiredness that is a result of "impure" blood.

Bronchial-Tee: this tea helps to relieve inflammation of the air passages and relieves in the elimination of phlegm.

Diabetiker-Tee: in general, recommended as a supplement to the doctor's care in the treatment of diabetic patients.

Entfettungs-Tee or *Schlankheits-Tee*: this weight-reducing tea works to withdraw the excess fat from the intestinal tract into the bowels, preventing its disposition in the form of fat on the body.

Harnsäure-Tee: this so-called uric acid tea is recommended for people with arthritis and rheumatism as it is believed to prevent the formation of uric acid crystals that form in the joints and cause pain.

Nerven-Tee für Frauen: this nerve tea is believed to be especially beneficial for women and particularly young women during menstruation and in general helps dissipate the accompanying disturbances such as headache, backache, and a general sick feeling.

Nieren-und-Blasen Tee: this kidney and bladder tea stimulates the regularity of the kidneys and strengthens them, dissolves salt in the urine, and prevents a buildup of stones and grit in the kidneys.

There are thirty commonly used Komplex Kräuter-Teesonten packaged by any one of several companies and available on the shelves of the Drogerie.

It is impossible to assess the specific medicinal claims made in support of the use of these many different herbal teas. Since all of them contain chemical substances found in nature, they may have some physiological effect. However, the actual amount of any such substances consumed, except by the most avid of tea drinkers, must be minute.

No one interviewed denied all efficacy to the Heilkräuter-Tee. They are used by families of all income and education levels, though not to the same extent in all families. Even the families of three interviewed doctors used teas rather extensively, and all three doctors indicated that they often recommended tea as a part of their treatment. Heilkräuter-Tee is also served in hospitals with meals, and many dentists prescribe camomile tea for patients who have had dental work.

Whatever their medical effect, there are substantial ritual elements in tea drinking. Many of the remedies such as the "blood-cleaning" tea are taken at only certain times of the year as an almost ceremonial seasonal observance. Other teas are consumed only at certain times of the day or only after or before certain meals or in association with certain foods. Even the association of specific teas with specific disorders may be considered ritualistic in character. Preparation of the various teas also involves considerable ritual. Some insist that the tea must be boiled with the water and then strained. Others say that the water must be boiled first and then poured on the tea, and some will never boil the water but rather let the tea steep in cool water overnight. Each method of preparation has its separate justification. These are self-verifying beliefs and ritualized behaviors that constitute an elaboration of means to an empirically unknown end. The ritual elements may indeed be the most important contribution to the assumed effect of the teas just as is the ritual of the therapeutic bath. The ritualized means produce the satisfaction. And again, the teas, like all forms of Volksheilkunde, make some kind of action possible from within the household to protect and succor its members.

General Attitudes toward Health and Disease

The people of Burgbach and the surrounding vicinity are very concerned about health and bodily functions. What one eats and drinks is considered important as well as how much exercise one gets and how much fresh air one breathes. Natural foods and natural exercise are considered good and beneficial to general health and well-being. Whereas Americans tend to be weight conscious, the people of Burgbach seem to be "health and nature" conscious. Attitudes toward disease and the treatment of illness and injury also seem to be quite different in the two cultural contexts. To the American student fresh from the aspirin-seltzer-antihis-tamine-antibiotic complex, not only the ordinary citizens of Burgbach but also German medical personnel seem very cautious about treatment of illness or injury. American students in Germany often complain that they "get nothing" from the doctors they go to with ordinary ailments or even with what seems to them a serious condition such as flu. Some students who have suffered broken limbs or other bodily injury have complained that the period of confinement to bed and to a hospital is much longer than they would have had to endure at home. Be that as it may, it is true that the medical personnel interviewed expressed doubts about the desirability of heavy treatment such as the prescription of antibiotics, except when they were absolutely necessary, and indicated that all such radical interventions in the natural functioning of the body constituted a severe physiological jolt. They felt that more natural ways of recovering were more desirable.

An emphasis upon nature and natural processes underlies many of the specific values and practices expressed in Volksheilkunde. As the author of one of the books that many families keep in the house for ready reference wrote, "He who trusts nature has not built on sand" (Roff 1956). Or consider the following comment from an advertising brochure from the Burgbach Fruit Juice Manufacturing Plant.

Out of nature continually comes much that is good. We all need a natural way of life. Only a very few people are still directly bound to nature. Only a few still work in the air and sun and live correctly. . . .

It is certain—we are all caught up in the spider web of modern civilization and cannot live as exceptions to this life. We nevertheless have the opportunity to live more naturally without leaving the job and losing time. We may introduce into our bodies materials which come out of the great store of power in nature. Doctors and scientists have firmly established that through the use of apples, elimination problems as well as liver and kidney disorders are favorably influenced.

We may not measure the worth of nutritional stuffs alone according to calories, proteins, vitamins, and other materials, but must also note the harmonious order in which they are contained in the means of nourishment.

Nature created structures in the organs of plants which have a definite purpose. . . .

This orientation toward nature and natural processes runs deep in the culture of the Remstal and probably deep in German culture as a whole. People keep plants in the living and dining rooms as they are thought to contribute to the purity of the air. People take walks in high places in the forest on the ridges or through the vineyards in order to get the fresh wind and better air.

This generalized orientation is reinforced by a "school" of medicine that has been practiced in Europe and to some extent in North America for some time—the homeopathic school. The fundamental precept of this school is that recovery from illness must be through the natural processes of the body, and that the function of medication should be to stimulate these processes. Surgery or strong drugs such as antibiotics should only be taken in case of emergency when the body appears incapable of healing itself, or with the aid of natural medications in small doses. Drugs may be administered but only in infinitesimally small amounts to trigger natural bodily functions.

The homeopathic orientation certainly cannot be said to dominate modern German medical practice, but some of the continuity between medical practice and Volksheilkunde may be in part due to the influence of this school of medical practice. In any event, there seems to be an internally coherent pattern that includes some parts of contemporary medical practice as well as folk belief and practice. However, the coherence of the pattern neither validates nor challenges the validity of either folk or professional medical practice.

The culture pattern we are considering here is demonstrated by the results of an interview with one family. The male head of the house is a lawyer. Both he and his wife are university educated and are sophisticated people. The doctor is not called in this household until it is clear that the illness is beyond the ability of ordinary household treatment to handle. Frau Kahn, as we will call her, says that she likes to use natural cures. Rest, a good bath, and some tea are about all that one needs for most illnesses since the body cures itself. If one of the children is feeling a bit low, she will give him or her one of the several teas that she uses habitually and tells the child to lie down. If it looks as if a cold is developing, camomile tea will be taken because it loosens the bronchial tubes and allows drainage, Frau Kahn says. If there is a sore throat, gargling with hot lemon juice and honey or hot salt water is recommended, and if there is a stomachache involved, a warm towel is placed on the stomach and one drinks camomile or peppermint tea or both. Above all, one must stay in bed and keep warm and avoid all chilling. Even if a fever may appear, the use of antiobiotics is not anticipated. Frau Kahn says that the body builds up resistance to antibiotics and that when they are really needed, they no longer help. She says that even aspirin is too harsh and is unnecessary. If it looks as if there is a serious case of grippe, or one of the several common childhood diseases, the doctor will be called. Usually the doctor, according to Frau Kahn, recommends more tea, more rest, sweating, and staying in bed until all symptoms disappear. As the patient recovers from either the common cold or the childhood diseases, he or she will continue to get warm tea but also may choose from any combination of possibilities from the many *Säfte*—apple juice, grape juice, orange juice, currant juice, carrot juice, and so on—with or without mineral water.

Families with less education and with a life style closer to that of the more traditional Weingärtner-Bauer culture differ from the family just described mainly in the greater extent to which home remedies are used, the high degree of specificity concerning the relationship between treatment, disease, and cure, and reliance upon what appears to be a great amount of ritualization of the kind described in previous sections. The goal is the same—life and health. The Volksheilkunde remedies are rituals that produce auxiliary satisfactions and are self-sustaining because they do.

Final Comments on Volksheilkunde

Cultural continuity is the theme of this chapter. We are concerned with some of the ways in which there is continuity with the past in Burgbach (and Remstal) culture and with some of the processes that support this continuity. In the first section we dealt with the reaffirmation of identity expressed in the yearly Kirbe-fest. In this section we have discussed Volksheilkunde, a cultural complex center-ing upon disease and its cures. The widespread use of Volksheilkunde in Remstal homes is a direct expression of cultural persistence. Volksheilkunde is of very long standing, reaching well back in time to the Middle Ages and in forms specifically represented in the present pattern. This complex of attitudes and values, beliefs and practices, as we have seen, is related to an orientation toward nature and natural life processes that extends beyond folk or professional medical practice into other patterns and sectors of behavior. The general orientation toward nature and health and the specific health practices support each other and in so doing, constitute a significant process of cultural continuity.

We may look tentatively beyond these direct relationships to some indirect functions of Volksheilkunde. These practices make possible the treatment of minor illness and injury in the home and family that therefore provide a sense of security that reinforces the familial orientation we have already discussed. Volksheilkunde is another way in which the family insulates and protects the individual from the threatening world outside. Familial values thus strengthened may in turn support a relatively conservative cultural orientation in the midst of an urbanizing, modernizing environment, providing that the family and its child-training environment are slower to adapt to changed conditions than other institu-tions and practices, or if the family transmits and reinforces values that · are incongruent with full social participation in the outside world. We have some evidence that the values of parents of children in our elementary school sample are culturally conservative (see Chapter 6). Dahrendorf (1967) also argues that the familial, private values in German society are a block to full scale public participation and the taking of responsibility for public values, and that the family has precedence over the school.

Whatever its indirect functions, it appears that Volksheilkunde is becoming weaker. Drogisten who have been in the business for more than twenty years said that the decline in the use of medicinal herbal tea was substantial, particularly during the last ten years. All cultural persistence is, however, relative to varying rates of change. As seen from the American observers' point of view, the survival of Volksheilkunde is more impressive than its decline.

Lastly, we should take note of the fact that we have not been discussing a culture pattern limited to Burgbach, the Remstal, Baden-Württemberg, southern Germany, or even to Europe. Volksheilkunde is found in some form throughout Europe and, in attenuated form, in America as well. It should also be clear that we are not taking the supercilious position that American attitudes toward health and disease are less ritualized or more sophisticated than German attitudes or Burgbach attitudes. The American who goes to the doctor with a severe cold, demanding an antibiotic for a "virus" may be thinking magically. He may well be less sophisticated in his reasoning than the user of Volksheilkunde who has a clear rationale in mind about the relationship between illness, treatment, and bodily processes. Ritual elements are present in all medical practice, folk or professional. The important point in our analysis is that a whole system of beliefs and practices concerning health and disease, a very basic area of human thinking and behavior, has survived in complex form and constitutes a major cultural continuity in the community we are studying. It has survived partly because it is ritualized and self-verifying. That it helps validate the family, home, and parental care as an indirect function may also be significant.

We now turn to quite a different force for cultural persistence, and yet one that also exhibits the self-verifying process and the results of ritualization.

ECOLOGICAL "LOCK-IN"

In this section we are concerned with the ways in which the particular adaptation made to the land, the forms of agricultural production, and the kind and location of the residences of those who use the land, together form a complex and unwieldly pattern that constitutes a kind of "lock-in" within and between the various elements. All cultural systems have developed various forms of ecological "lock-in" though they are most obvious in stabilized and technologically simple cultural systems. Burgbach no longer has a simple cultural system and the interdependencies between man, land, and culture have correspondingly become more complex. Nevertheless, a complex of interdependent adaptations still survives centering on the cultivation of wine grapes, the large Bauernhäuser, size and distribution of plots, relationships between members of families, technical equipment and uses of it, and other aspects of the traditional land-based culture of the Remstal.

The complex we are describing has persisted for a long time. Some of its elements must have first appeared during the Roman occupation, for the Romans brought the art of wine making and of vine cultivation with them to the Remstal. The "lock-in" we are describing did not develop fully, however, until the latter part of the Middle Ages. During the thirteenth, fourteenth, and fifteenth centuries the Remstal lands were cleared and drained and the pattern of small plot agriculture became stabilized. Inheritance of lands by the oldest son (primogeniture)

Traditional Weinberge. Each terrace marks a separate plot owned by different people. This is a significant factor in "ecological lock-in." The shelter is a tool shed and resting place. (Courtesy Brian Mittelstaedt and Susan Talbot.)

was not practiced. The lands were divided among all the children and the plots became smaller and smaller.

As one looks at the *Ortsplan* (village layout) of Burgbach with the Bauernhäuser identified, one is impressed by the fact that there is no concentration of these houses in any single part of the village (see Figure 2, p. 82). An active Bauernhaus may be right next to a very modern apartment house or business establishment. There has been a physical integration that is only partly represented in social integration. But Burgbach has avoided the situation of many rapidly expanding villages such as Rebhausen (Warren 1967) where the traditional Bauernhäuser are in one area and the "new town" of Zugezogenen in another. It is difficult to say precisely what effect this may have had upon political and social behavior in Burgbach as contrasted to other villages. That it had some influence in the direction of greater social integration seems probable.

In 1960, when the distribution and character of the Bauernhäuser were first studied by Stanford students, there were 116 that still housed animals and agricultural equipment as well as people. Today (as of April 1970), there are only 86 such houses still active as participating units in the agricultural-Weingärtner enterprise.[6] There are another eighty renovated houses that can be identified both from recent records and inspection as former Bauernhäuser. Some serve as large single-family dwellings, others as duplexes or apartment houses, and a few have

---

[6] Our latest count, as of May 1972, reveals only fifty-four active Bauernhäuser.

been modified as business establishments. Another undetermined number have been demolished in the process of constructing new buildings. We will describe two of the Bauernhäuser that are still used in the traditional fashion and the activities that take place within them. The way of life based on vineyards, orchards, and meadow plots on the slopes and on the flatlands is ancient. The total set of relationships described constitutes an ecological "lock-in" that is not easily changed and that constitutes a major force supporting cultural continuity in Burgbach.

The cows are in a side room on the ground floor. (Courtesy Rick Hanson.)

We will call the family occupying one Bauernhaus Schmid and the other Hünle. Both families live in what Americans would call the second and third stories of their great houses. The first, the ground floor, is used to store machinery, hay, and grain, and to house the animals. A root cellar in which various root crops for men and animals are stored opens directly from this floor. On this floor there also is a large room that opens directly on the street, with full-length double doors. Wagons and tractors are driven in here, sometimes with full loads of hay. The hayloft fills one side of the "barn" extending to the roof, which in the loft area is the same height as the roof of the house. The cows and other livestock are kept in another side room accessible by a door which opens only from the main room. Herr Schmid has three cows, four pigs, usually a calf or two, and about a dozen laying hens. Herr Hünle keeps two cows, three pigs, eight laying hens, usually a calf, and six or seven rabbits. Altogether in Burgbach there are 160 cows, 150 pigs, and 700 chickens.[7] No one knows just how many rabbits there are.

Both families own plots in the flat valley area, and vineyard, orchard, and meadow plots on the slopes. The Schmid family works six Weinberge. The largest

---

[7] This figure was derived from a count in February 1967. There are fewer Bauernhäuser housing livestock today (May 1972).

is .45 of an acre in size and the smallest is .09 of an acre. They also have thirteen flatland and three orchard plots. None of these pieces are larger than .60 of an acre. The total land owned and utilized for agricultural purposes by the Schmid family is 8.84 acres. The Hünle family has about the same distribution of plots, and owns and works a total of 9.3 acres. Both are above the average of 5.95 acres for those who own and work the land in the Burgbach *Gemeinde* as a significant part of their subsistence.[8]

Most of the plots for both families are not contiguous with each other and are distributed over a wide area in the Gemeinde (see Figure 2, p. 82). The absence of a rule of primogeniture (inheritance by the oldest heir) has resulted in a splintering of all of the plots into tiny pieces scattered over a wide area. The Schmid and Hünle families also own some Weinberge in the area of a neighboring village. This is not uncommon and, in fact, about a quarter of the workable land in the Burgbach Gemeinde is owned by people living in neighboring villages. This, too, is the result of the inheritance pattern. The small size of the plots and their wide spatial distribution means that the members of the Schmid and Hünle families must travel about to get their work done. Since the plots are so small, it also means that only mechanized equipment and techniques suitable for very small plots can be utilized. This is the key to the ecological "lock-in."

The Schmid and Hünle families grow food for both animals and humans on their flatland plots, including wheat, oats, barley, turnips, potatoes, cabbages, red beets, carrots, green beans, celery, onions, spices, and herbs. In the orchard plots (*Obstgärten*) there are apple, pear, cherry, plum, and apricot trees. Grasses which are used for cow fodder grow among the trees. These grasses are not planted, but grow wild. Black currants and strawberry plants also grow in tiny plots scattered both on the orchard land and on the flatland. Two types of corn are also raised on the flatland: one for chickens and the other for cows. Corn is not regarded as human food. Each family also has small plots of hillside meadow where alfalfa or mixed hay is raised and cut for the cows.

The flatland plots (*Äcker*) vary in size. Grains are planted in the larger, flatter plots while root crops, corn, berries, and garden vegetables are raised in the smaller ones. Crop rotation is practiced. For example, root crops will be grown for one year; the second, wheat; the third, oats or barley. The Weinberge are also split into many small separated plots. It is clear that the Schmid and Hünle families are engaged in growing many different crops on many different spatially separated little plots of land, each requiring specialized operations.

The animals also take time and require special care. The cows are fed the same diet morning and night just before they are milked. Each cow gets one bushel of chopped turnips, one liter of ground oats and barley (in the winter), and one liter of protein concentrate plus a handful of chalk powder for calcium. In the summer, the cows enjoy fresh chopped corn including kernel, cob, and stock as a substitute for the ground oats and barley of the winter. During the summer, they also get fresh grass that is cut every two days and hauled to them by tractor and

---

[8] *Gemeinde* must be used here rather than "community" because we refer to the whole geographic area of Burgbach, including all kinds of lands as well as the village itself.

wagon. The cows themselves never leave the Bauernhaus. Only one of the cows in these two families has ever been outdoors. In the winter the cows have all the hay they can eat all day long.

The pigs must also be fed morning and evening. When they are very young they eat only potatoes which are cooked in a special pan over a gas flame. As they get older, the potatoes are cooked less and less. When the pigs are two months old they also get coarsely ground oats and wheat, and a protein concentrate. The amount of food increases as the pig gets older. Table scraps are also given to the pigs when there are any.

When they are mature the chickens eat wheat, oats, barley, and corn, all coarsely ground. Baby chicks eat only very finely ground grains. The older chickens also get corn-on-the-cob, which has first been dried, as well as a fish meal and protein concentrate. The rabbits are fed greens, grains, and occasional leftovers from the family table.

Under the living quarters in both of the houses is a large work area where tools and machinery are kept, including those used for the care of the grape vines, the gathering of grain, and the repairing of tools, and the larger machines such as the mower and tractor. There are many different kinds of hand tools hung on the walls. The number and kinds of these tools, such as rakes, hoes, scythes, and spades, give the impression of a very complex operation.

In the barn near the cow stall in Herr Schmid's Bauernhaus there is an electric turnip chopper. Knives whirl around inside the hopper and chop the turnips into square pieces approximately a cubic inch large. Herr Schmid throws the turnips into the chopper after having first cut them into pieces approximately three inches by three inches with a small hand ax. The chopped turnips fall out of the bottom of the hopper and are caught in a bushel basket. In Herr Hünle's work area next to the electric turnip chopper there is an old chopper that is run by hand. It works on exactly the same principle as the new one.

In Herr Schmid's ground floor there is a fodder cutter which chops hay into cow-bite-size pieces. Hay is fed into one side of the machine, taken through the knives, and expelled out the other side. Herr Hünle says that it is unnecessary to chop the hay for the cows at all.

Both Herr Schmid and Herr Hünle have the same type of land-tilling machine similar to a rototiller in America. It has a combination of plow-and-disc blades which are rotated by a small diesel motor. The machines are small enough to fit in the narrow rows between the grape vines on the steep hillsides and are guided by a man or women. Some of the Weinberge are too steep even for these machines and must be worked entirely by hand.

Both families also own a mowing machine which is about the same size as the rototiller, except for the blade which is approximately 3 feet long. These machines are also "garden-tractor" size and are guided by a walking man or woman. It is clear that the field and Weinberg equipment, even though powered, is adapted to the special lay of the land and particularly to the small plots.

Each of the families also has an apple-masher which is powered by electricity. The apples are placed on a plate which has prongs on it that rotates in turn against other pronged plates, mashing the apples. Juice flows out of a spout and

Rototillers are used between the rows of wire-supported grapevines. (Courtesy Rick Hanson.)

Tractors are used to haul wagons and equipment to and from the Weinberge. (Courtesy Rick Hanson.)

the mashed apple residue collects in a pot to be used for apple sauce or fed to the animals. As in the case of the turnip-chopper, a similar hand-powered machine was used until recently. One of these stands in the corner at Herr Hünle's. There are also several sets of harrows and plows in each of the Bauernhäuser. The old ones, now unused, were pulled by the cows. The new ones are pulled by the tractor and can only be used on the flat Äcker on the valley floor. Each of the families has a new wagon with pneumatic rubber ties which is used for hauling most everything excepting manure. This is hauled in the old wagons that were at one time pulled by the cows.

The largest and most expensive single piece of equipment owned by each of the families is the tractor, which runs on diesel fuel. Herr Schmid has had his for ten years, and Herr Hünle has had his for three years. The tractors are used for two main purposes: to plow (but not to cultivate) the flatland plots and to pull wagons with people, tools, and materials such as manure, up to and around the various small plots located some distance from each other. The tractors make it possible to get around more quickly. They do not essentially change the nature of the operation.

The area of both houses that is devoted to tools and equipment contains the usual conglomeration of old and new, broken and whole, dirty and clean, pieces of equipment and implements. In the main rooms hang ladders, hay racks, rakes, stakes, and boards for repairing wagons. In the spaces between the ladder rungs and hanging from nails are cans filled with nuts and bolts, bottles filled with oil, grease, and turpentine, paint cans and brushes, rags, pieces of twine used to tie grape twig bundles together, cotton string used to bind grain shocks, and aprons and lengths of chain.

Tools are hung from the rafters. Herr Schmid has five scythes and Herr Hünle has four. Eight different kinds of hoes are hung from the rafters of Herr Schmid's working area. Some have broad short heads for shallow hoeing. Some have long broad heads for deeper working of the soil. Some are pronged for finer work. Others are long and narrow and are used to uproot plants and clean out weeds. There are six different kinds of shovels in Herr Schmid's barn, and five in Herr Hünle's. There are square ones used for cleaning stalls and for working the soil around the borders in the small plots. There are pointed ones used for digging or spading. There are scoop shovels. There are also several kinds of pitchforks standing against the walls. They are used to clean the cow stalls, scatter straw bedding, fork hay in and out of the wagons and down to the cows so they can eat it, and formerly to load grain schocks into wagons and into threshing machines. Three different kinds of axes and two types of hatchets are also found in each of the barn areas. There are ten wooden rakes hanging from the rafters in Herr Schmid's barn area. Some are used for spreading manure in the orchards, raking hay into piles, and for raking swathed grain.

In the cow stalls stand twig brooms used to sweep the straw and manure into a pile. Homemade twig brooms are used because they are stronger and last longer than the straw brooms sold in stores, according to both Herr Schmid and Herr Hünle. A curry comb and brush sit on a window ledge and are used to clean the cows. There are wooden milk stools in the stalls.

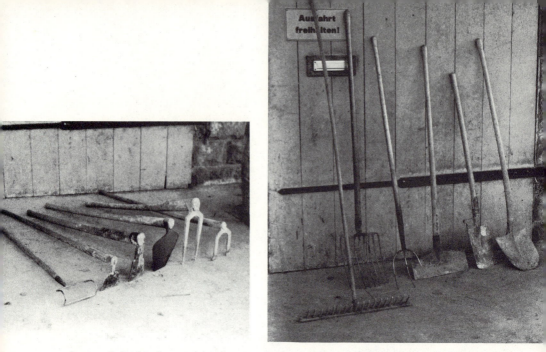

*Some of the implements used to work the soil by hand. (Courtesy Melvin Malinow-
ski, Tim McCoy, and Charles Thumin.)*

*The wooden bucket on its frame, of the type used to carry earth, manure, or grapes.
(Courtesy Tim McCoy.)*

In the work area there are bushel baskets made from reeds. They are used to hold turnips and potatoes and other foods taken to the animals. A wooden milk cart stands ready to be pulled by a member of the family to the milk cooperative. It is also used to take dough in pans to the bake house and the bread back home again. There is a wooden wheelbarrow used to carry manure out of the stall to the Mist pile just outside the house near the street. There are also several high, narrow, wooden baskets with shoulder straps so that they can be carried on the back. They are supported by a wooden frame. Some are used to carry manure and dirt about in the Weinberge. For generations people have combatted erosion in the Weinberge by carrying dirt from the lower to the upper areas on their backs. Other similar baskets are used to put the grapes in during harvest and carry them to the collecting wagon.

There is always something to do around the Bauernhaus or out on the land. In November after the grapes are harvested, the land in the Weinberge is spaded and manure is spread. The vines are stretched out on the ground and fastened down by a large iron staple which looks like a croquet wicket. This is intended as protection against freezing. The youngest vines are covered with dirt as protection against the cold. The younger Weingärtner, however, do not do this, possibly because recent winters have been mild. During November, also, the grain stubble on the flatland plots is plowed under and barley is planted in late December for harvest in June.

Manure is taken up to the Weinberge and out to the Äcker as it accumulates in the Mist pile in both solid and liquid form. Grape stakes are prepared and new trellises are built so as to be ready for the spring.

In February the snow, if there has been any, melts and the vines and trees are pruned. This work continues until April and requires the cooperation of the whole family. The grape vines, too, must be tied into a circle so that many new branches will grow out from it. This must be done in the early morning when the vines are wet and the twigs are flexible.

In April the Äcker are plowed (or in March if the weather permits), and oats and wheat are planted, as are turnips and potatoes and the various kitchen vegetables. The grapevines and the fruit trees must also be sprayed now. If the spring is wet, the vines must be sprayed five times or more, once a week from April to May. If the spring is dry, spraying is done only twice. The fruit trees are only sprayed twice, once for the blossoms and once for the new fruit.

During the summer months the Weinberge must be cared for continually. The soil is loosened occasionally, and the weeds are removed. Some of the younger Weingärtner use weed killers. Some of the older ones insist this is not good for the grapes and remove the weeds by hand. The flatland plots must also be tended, as the various crops and garden vegetables come in at different times and must be harvested, and the plots must be weeded and cultivated.

In October there is the harvest of the grapes, the *Weinlese*. Everybody joins in though the work must be done carefully. Using a small pair of clippers the grapes are picked by hand with usually one to three bunches on each of the stems. The grapes are first collected in back-carried wooden baskets and then taken to the waiting wagon. The wagon takes them to a local collecting point and eventually to the Remstal winery. Here the weight of the grapes brought in by each owner is recorded before the grapes are pressed into juice. The actual process of wine making, which is quite complex and requires careful controls for standard quality, is out of the hands of the Weingärtner. Though both the Schmid and Hünle families make enough wine themselves for their own use, only a few of the older Weingärtner actually do this now.

In the Schmid and Hünle families there is surprisingly little food purchased. All of the vegetables eaten are raised on the garden plots. Both families use their own ground wheat for bread and Kuchen, their own fruit for juices and cider, and their own grapes for wine. Cows furnish the necessary milk and the creamery makes butter from some of it. Chickens furnish eggs. The feed for the animals is raised on the flatland plots. Only the protein concentrate, chalk powder, and fish meal must be bought. The straw of the grain is used for bedding. Both families raise all of their own fruit, much of which is canned for the winter months. Both still burn a considerable amount of wood which they can obtain from the common area owned by the Gemeinde although both also buy some coal as well as diesel and gasoline fuel.

Surplus fruit is sold as are eggs and milk. The grapes are the important cash crop, however.

Interpretation

The Schmid and Hünle families and their activities, possessions, and Bauernhäuser are representative of the traditional agricultural adaptation in Burgbach. The newer style of Weingärtner is more specialized and many do not keep animals or even use manure. In their operations these newer style Weingärtner represent the effects of the rationalization of agriculture. We have selected the Schmid and Hünle adaptation as more characteristic of the past and as representing in most clear form the survival of that past into the present. Certain features stand out clearly in this adaptation.

There are many different crops, each requiring specialized operations. This is time consuming and economically unproductive. A total community of men, animals, plants, and soil interacts in this pattern. As long as the Weingärtner receives the larger part of his family's food from this operation it seems to make sense. But careful bookkeeping reveals that this is an illusion, at least under the conditions that have prevailed since 1945, and probably well before that. Agronimists tell the farmer and Weingärtner that it is better to concentrate on one or two cash crops. Nor does it pay to keep livestock on the traditional basis. They require special foods that must be grown with soil, fertilizer, energy, and time which could be converted more directly into cash through single-crop production. It becomes clear that the total pattern we have described is no longer rational, and has not been for some time. The ritual of growing food for one's own table has been, however, a persistent block against fully professional specialization. As one man said when advised to focus entirely on wine-grape production, "Where would I get my potatoes?"

There are many specialized tools and much handling of the various grains, vegetables, and fruits. For example, in the case of the turnips fed to cows, as we have explained, they must first be planted and cultivated, then harvested and brought to the Bauernhaus. There they must be removed from the wagon and stored until used. When used, they are first cut into medium-sized chunks and then put into a machine by hand that chops them into smaller pieces. They must, in turn, be collected from the machine and carried to the cows who eat them. Each product or food production element requires a chain of operations as complex as this. It is no wonder that the Weingärtner and his wife must get up before dawn and rarely go to bed until late during the busy season. This unceasing labor was invested with high moral value, thus justifying the ritualized operations that made it necessary.

Most of the operations one carried out by hand or by back work. Not only must fine types of work such as pruning grape vines be done by hand but also even gross activities such as cultivation, turning the earth by spading (rather than plowing) and carrying dirt.

Motorization, the substitution of mechanized power units for human and animal power units, is sharply limited by plot size and distribution of plots.[9] The rototiller and the hay cutter are good examples. Though motorization has speeded up an activity, the activity itself has not changed essentially. The rototiller is nothing more than a mechanized hoe. And this is even more clear in the instances of the turnip choppers and apple press. Machines identical in principle are now run by electric motors that were once run by hand. This is substitutive change. The operation is made easier but does not change essentially.

The same general process of nontransformative, substitutive change can be seen in the case of the tractor. A large number of tractors were acquired rather suddenly by the Bauern after World War II. Where there had been cows drawing wagons about the streets of Burgbach and out to the flat Äcker and up to the Weinberge, there were now tractors pulling the same wagons, with the same materials, people, and equipment in them to do the same things once they arrived at their destination. The basic pattern of activity had not changed. The tractor was merely substituted for the cow and made the operation somewhat quicker. The most important use of the tractor was to permit the Bauer and his family to get from one piece of land to another more rapidly.

The motorization that did occur can be said to have not only been substitutive rather than transformative but also can be regarded as one of the factors keeping the traditional pattern intact. The traditional pattern could be maintained longer in the face of an increasing shortage of low cost labor because the operations required within it could be carried out more quickly because of motorization. The limiting factor appears to be the size and the distribution of the plots, as well as the inertia of the complex of self-subsistence. Until some major intervention in the relationship of man, animals, equipment, land, and produce could occur,

---

[9] "Motorization" is used rather than "mechanization" because the latter implies a more total conversion to powered, mechanized operations than is implied by the former.

there was little likelihood that this complex pattern of activities would be changed in any essential way. The complex operations, as they are carried out in the two situations described, are nonrational, that is, they developed as patterns through the accumulation of usages based upon an essentially subsistence economy and a basic ecological limitation—the size and distribution of plots—that was, in turn, a function of a social process, an inheritance pattern. This nonrational complex is highly ritualized, that is, its various elements had become sources of satisfaction in themselves, irrespective of their nonutility under changing circumstances.

Old people who have worked on the land all their lives say they liked working with the hoe and spade. They value the terraces built of heavy stones by back-breaking labor. They take pride in the handwork necessary to prune and support the vines. They spend many hours tying vines in one of several ways, no one of which has positive controlled evidence to support its usage; and more hours tying vine clippings in neat bundles that are almost exactly the same length and circumference, only to burn them in the baking ovens or start cooking fires with them. Modern Weingärtner have their rituals too, as all craftsmen do, for example the building of wonderfully precise wire and pole trellises that would take less time if they were less precise. Their rituals have not as yet developed to the point where they are a serious impediment to the new rationalization however.

Within the framework of a partially subsistence-oriented economy with a plentiful labor supply the pattern described developed as an adaptation to conditions as they existed, including the inheritance pattern that caused more and more splintering of the land. But these adaptations came to have value in themselves and became impediments to change. When self-subsistence became irrelevant and when time as well as labor became precious commodities the whole pattern with its ritualized elements became nonrational and dysfunctional. It has persisted into the present partly because it has provided ancillary satisfactions, but also because only substitutive changes were made in the whole complex. These substitutive changes, such as the electric motor on the turnip chopper and the tractor in place of the cow used for drayage helped make it possible for the complex to survive even though it was nonrational under the changing circumstances. Probably some such interpretations are relevant wherever established economic and technological systems are faced with changing conditions.

Hauptberuflich und Nebenberuflich

We have described a way of life in its more traditional rather than its more progressive form, but all of the individuals who list themselves as Weingärtner on the *Meldungskarten* (information cards) in the Rathaus have some connection with this culture complex. There is also a larger number of people who maintain a connection with the land and with the activities associated with its cultivation. Those who are full-time Weingärtner (there are none in Burgbach who are simply farmers and not also Weingärtner) are *hauptberuflich* Weingärtner—that is, professional vinters. Those who merely keep "einen Fuss am Boden" one foot on the land, who have only a small piece of land that they cultivate but who make their living by other means, are classed as *nebenberuflich* (part time). Together these two groups constitute a significant portion of the gainfully employed persons in Burgbach. They are the core of the einheimisch community and constitute that part of the population of Burgbach that exhibits the greatest continuity with the past.

Just how large is this group of professional and part-time Weingärtner? This question has not proven easy to answer. Being a Weingärtner has prestige value, so many people write "Weingärtner" on their personal information card where profession or trade is asked for, even though they receive the greatest part of their subsistence from some other source. Indirect data and interpolation must be utilized.

There are 240 people living in Burgbach who own Weinberge, and the only people who own Weinberge, with the exception of three migrants married to Burgbach women, are natives. However, only 96 people list themselves as Weingärtner on the information cards. An examination of the amount of land owned, however, indicates that only 34 of these own more than one acre of Weinberg and it is not probable that one can be a professional Weingärtner with less than one acre. Actually, approximately four acres of Weinberge is necessary, but we are making allowance for certain factors, including ownership of other types of agricultural land in these cases. We may infer that at least 62 of the people who list themselves as Weingärtner are actually part-timers. But we have a total group of 240 people who own Weinberge. If we subtract from that figure the originally listed 96 Weingärtner, we have 144 who are probably part-timers. If we add to that figure the 62 listed as Weingärtner but owning less than one acre of Weinberg, we have a total of 206 persons who are in some way connected with the Weinberge and with wine-grape cultivation, even though they are not deriving their main subsistence from it, in addition to the 34 who are ostensibly full-time Weingärtner.

Where do these people live in Burgbach? As stated previously, there are at present 86 active Bauernhäuser and about 80 that can be regarded as recently active but now inactive. There are 96 families living in the 86 active Bauernhäuser. The heads of at least 60 of these families earn their main livelihood as masons, truck drivers, mechanics, barrel makers, bank clerks, and so forth. In addition, they work on the Weinberge. And 5 of the most active Weingärtner do not live in Bauernhäuser at all, although members of their extended family do. These 86 active Bauernhäuser constitute a significant and highly visible part of Burgbach, amounting to about 8 percent of the total number of buildings of any kind in the village.

The distribution of Bauernhäuser within the village (see Figure 2) in relationship to the widely distributed plots of flatland (Äcker), vineyards (Weinberge), and orchards (Obstgärten), constitute the ecological unit that we have been describing.[10] The distribution of Bauernhäuser and the distribution of plots bear

[10] This is a schematic, rather than realistic map intended to show relationships among the elements of the "ecological lock-in."

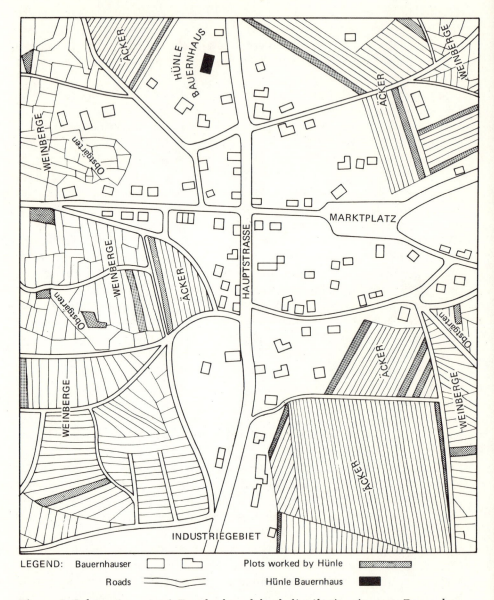

Figure 2. Schematic map of Burgbach and land distribution for one Bauernhaus.

no rational relationship to each other. It is, in part, the very nonrationality of the total complex that has, as we have seen, kept it in operation for so long in almost unchanged form.

We return now to the question of the significance of the Weinberge-owning group. This category includes full-time Weingärtner, part-time Weingärtner, and people who have only a token relationship to the cultivation of wine grapes. In the total distribution of occupations in Burgbach we find that they constitute together a definitely significant group. The occupational distribution of Burgbach, excluding Weingärtner, is given below.

OCCUPATIONAL DISTRIBUTION IN BURGBACH

	Percent		Percent
Akademiker (qualified officials and professionals)	3.4	*Angestellte* (white-collar workers)	26.5
Grosshändler (big businessmen)	.3	*Handwerker* (skilled workers)	14.0
Beamte (Civil servants and professionals)	3.0	*Arbeiter* (semi- and unskilled workers)	29.5
Technische Berufe (technical professions)	10.0	*Haushelferinnen* (household helpers)	5.0
Kaufleute (small businessmen)	8.3		

Weingärtner, either professional or part-time, are left out of the above distribution. If we adjust our distribution to include the 96 declared Weingärtner, about 5 percent of the total number of gainfully employed persons in Burgbach are full-time Weingärtner. If we accept the previous analysis, less than 2 percent (34 persons) would be full-time Weingärtner. However, if we take the total number (206) of part-timers of all kinds together with the 34 presumed professionals,[11] we have a total of 240 persons. This means that there is potentially that number of persons in Burgbach who have some direct connection with the Weinberge, and indirectly at least, a connection with the way of life centering upon their use. There are also a number of people who own scattered pieces of orchard, meadow, or garden land who are not included in the above calculations. Seen in terms of proportionate occupational distributions in the table above, those related to the Weinberge in some way constitute one of the four largest occupational blocks, and a total representation of about 13 percent of the whole occupational distribution. This, of course, is an ambiguous even misleading, figure unless we keep our reservations in mind. As we have tried to make clear, by far the greatest number of those who own Weinberge are not professional Weingärtner.

It appears that the way of life that we have been describing is far from dead. The very fact that nearly all of the agricultural land is owned by Einheimischen, and that a large number of people who are not professional Weingärtner own Weinberge, as well as other agricultural land which we have not considered, suggests the strength of the "einen Fuss am Boden" orientation. There are, however, some processes under way that will have a decisive influence upon this picture. Even at present there are three families who own about 25 percent of all the agricultural land and approximately one third of the Weinberge in the Burgbach Gemeinde. And one family with twenty-six landowners in it owns almost

---

[11] We qualify the term "professional" or "full-time" because probably most of these 34 engage in seasonal employment of some kind. It is impossible to arrive at truly accurate figures.

half of the amount owned by the three families. There is little or no attrition with respect to the number of Weingärtner over three generations in these three families. In the largest land-owning family, of twenty-two individuals who could be Weingärtner, sixteen actually declare themselves to be. This is a "hard core" group which appears to be enlarging its holdings and professionalizing its operations. The amount of land held by families other than these three has tended to decrease. In the Burgbach Gemeinde as a whole 20 percent of the landowners own almost 80 percent of the land. Many families have, however, kept a few square meters of land in a tiny vineyard, garden, or orchard plot.

Most of the changes in the ownership of land and the shifts from full-time to part-time or to token viniculture have apparently taken place as the result of the sudden expansion of occupational alternatives consequent to the rapid industrialization and urbanization occurring after World War II. The impact of those processes will be described in the next chapter. We will also describe the process called Flurbereinigung—the legal and physical consolidation of Weinberge. This process hits most directly at the ecological "lock-in" that we have described.

Other Forces for Continuity

This chapter has dealt with forces for cultural continuity in Burgbach in four dimensions: reaffirmation of identity exemplified by the Kirbefest; self-verifying cultural patterns exemplified by Volksheilkunde; ritualization that is present in all the behavior patterns discussed; and the ecological "lock-in" created by the interrelationship of people, animals, land, and equipment within the limits placed upon them by the pattern of widely distributed small plots, with variagated and specialized crops.

There are other dynamics of cultural continuity that we have not discussed but that will be encountered indirectly in other contexts. The continued existence of the schwäbisch speech community deserves more attention here. It is in itself a most important form of cultural continuity. The subtle reinforcement of interpersonal attitudes and world view in this speech form and in the social interaction which occurs within its framework of meaning is very difficult to describe but is very palpable as one moves about in the Burgbach community, particularly as a stranger.

It is claimed that only those born in the schwäbisch speech can learn it. It can, of course, be learned as can any language. One elderly man said, however, "D'Lait, d'sprechet net mehr d'alt, d'echte reine Sprache" (The people no longer speak the old, genuine, clear speech.) And the schwäbisch "foster parents" of Stanford students thought that their adopted offspring who wanted to learn to speak Schwäbisch "haben Köpfle voller Mucke!" (have their heads full of nonsensical aspirations).

Schwäbisch is spoken with an up and down melody that is not communicated in the samples given above. It is also different in other specific ways. Many standard High German words are shortened and phonetically changed. There are also many standard German words that are used with altered meanings, many schwäbisch words that are not found in High German and many gender changes.

There are also grammatical differences, for example, the simple past tense is not used in Schwäbisch nor is the genitive case—the use of the latter would be considered arrogant.

There are significant regional differences within the schwäbisch speaking area. The area around Burgbach happens to be one where the dialect is least different from standard High German. There are also six different *Schichten,* or levels of language, within any part of Swabia: true folk speech; local slang; colloquial speech but not slang; "correct" or standardized *Honoratiorenschwäbisch*; Hochdeutsch spoken with a schwäbisch intonation; and *Bühnensprache,* Hochdeutsch spoken without accent ("stage speech").

The fact that dialect-free Hochdeutsch is known as a "stage speech" in southern Germany as elsewhere is a good indication of the true state of affairs. Schwäbisch is a "mother tongue" like the other regional dialects, a language of the natives—those who belong. It is taught in the home, learned from one's parents and other close relatives and friends, not at school from strange or forbidding preceptors. It is rich in the imagery of the Heimat, the homeland, and reminds one that the cultural history, and cultural difference, in this part of Germany stretch back through time to the early centuries of the Christian era. It is a Alemannen speech. The schwäbisch speech community persists, and in its persistence is a strong force for the persistence of values and attitudes, culturally reinforced characterological features, and ways of thinking that are traditionally Schwäbisch.

The schools are also forces for cultural continuity, though the schools in Burgbach are as "progressive" as any schools in similar communities, perhaps more so than most. Nevertheless, the schools, and particularly the Grundschule, operate as reaffirmation and recruitment agencies. They reaffirm the identity and validity of the community by teaching about its history and cultural features of the local area in Heimatkunde classes, and about the natural surroundings in Naturkunde lessons. They recruit the children into the existing community and into its social and occupational structure, or into similar structures elsewhere, wherever the children may eventually go as adults. We will describe and analyze what the schools do in Chapter 6.

The churches, and particularly the evangelische Kirche, also operate as forces for continuity since they tend to be conservative rather than *avante garde* in their orientation. The pride of many members of the community in the community itself constitutes another force for conservation of traditional values. The publication of the Heimatbuch and other brochures is a clear bid for a historical identity and is supportive of continuity.

There is much that appears to be working towards continuity in Burgbach. What forces are operating as influences toward discontinuity, change, and transformation? This is the subject of the next chapter.

5 / Transformation

Change in Burgbach has been a persistent theme in previous chapters. The presence of a new population from outside the Remstal is, by itself, both a major change and a cause of other changes. What these people brought with them in cultural background, dialects, education, religion, personal taste, and occupational skills, has created, as we saw in Chapters 2 and 3, complex diversity where there was relative uniformity.

In this chapter we are concerned with some of the most dramatic physical and cultural aspects of change represented in business and industrial development, and in the rationalization of agriculture. These changes are sufficiently dramatic to justify calling their totality a transformation. Physical changes in Burgbach, and changes in attitudes among the young, will be touched upon. The discussion of the rationalization process has been anticipated in Chapter 4, in the emphasis on ritualization and other nonrational components in agricultural production.

BUSINESS ESTABLISHMENTS

The new population coming into Burgbach not only brought new skills and cultural diversity with it, but also required jobs, accommodations and services far beyond those that the traditional community of Burgbach could supply. Factories, business establishments, and new housing were quickly built. Before the war there were forty business establishments of all kinds in the Burgbach Gemeinde including two factories, one devoted to the making of fruit juices and the other to the preparation of leather for finished goods. The *Remstalkellerei*, started in 1938, was also in operation by that time.[1] Between 1948 and 1970, fifty-four new business establishments were built, about two-thirds of them before 1960. These new business establishments include six new factories. The largest employs over 300 people. The goods and services produced by these fifty-four new business establishments cater to a population with increasingly diversified and sophisticated wants. A partial list of the types of enterprise follows:

[1] The *Remstalkellerei* is where grapes from Remstal communities are brought and processed into a variety of wines.

New construction on former agricultural flatland at the end of the village. (Courtesy Don Camp.)

Women's shoe factory, drug store (excluding prescriptive medication), medical office and business office equipment, grocery stores (four), express office, globe map factory, street construction materials, car rental, steel cabinet factory, precision machine products, mosaic and tile manufacturers, women's dressmaking shop, thermometer maker, transport contractors (two), textile material shop, cement delivery services, equipment distributor, caterer, sanitary installations, savings and loan associations, two laundries, a dry cleaner, two household electrical appliance shops, roll shutters installer, fancy stones importer, soft drinks distributor, fruit juice manufacturer and distributor, fashion studio, insurance company offices, upholstered furniture distributors and interior decorators, three building concerns.

Factories

The major factories include one that produces metal parts for autos; one that makes electrical and phone equipment, a major subsidiary of International Telephone and Telegraph; another that produces cabinets, desks, shelves, and technical furniture; a precision machine shop; a leather factory where leather is processed and tooled; and a globe factory.

All these factories require skilled handwork. The manufacture of world globes involves assembling and attaching by hand twelve molded and painted strips of metal as well as the preparation of the strips. The machined parts factory involves die casting and precision finishing. The metal furniture factory does only custom building of business and medical office furniture and equipment. The precision machine shop drills, grinds, and shapes machined tools or parts for larger firms. In the leather factory the leather pieces are processed and tooled in appropriate forms and styles for suitcases and purses. The Remstalkellerei, since it performs the whole process of wine making, involves a series of operations requiring a high degree of skill and technical knowledge.

These industries are characteristic of the Remstal area and help to account for the extraordinarily high level of prosperity enjoyed by it. In these factories there are 716 people employed of whom 230 are Burgbacher. Another 300 citizens of Burgbach work in the many other smaller business establishments, both old and new, but these same establishments employ over 100 people who do not live in Burgbach.

Commuting

There are approximately 1800 gainfully employed persons in the total Burgbach population. They engage in 334 different occupations subsumed under the nine major categories in Table 1, Chapter 4. However, excluding the Weingärtner, less than one fourth of the people in this working population work in Burgbach. The rest commute to their place of business or labor. The number of commuters has increased by over 100 percent during the decade 1960–1970. In 1948 there was only a handful of commuters.

Burgbach, once a village of Weingärtner, is clearly a community of high occupational diversity and skilled technical labor and production, but also very clearly a commuters' town, a Vorort. Indeed, Burgbach is not only a Vorort in the sense that the greatest share of the gainfully-employed leave each day to work some place else, but it is also a place where some 600 people come each day for their work. This means that around 2,000 people must enter and leave or leave and reenter the Burgbach Gemeinde each day. Though we have no accurate figures, it seems probable that about 40 percent is carried by public transportation, largely the railroad, and 60 percent by private means of conveyance including cars, motorcycles, motor scooters, and bicycles. Burgach has also become a parking lot and a traffic center. Accommodation to the automobiles that speed all too rapidly through the narrow streets of the village and to the cars that must be parked up on sidewalks and crammed into the parking areas of the Marktplatz is one of the significant features of life in today's Burgbach.

Changes in Attitude

With all of this, it is easy to forget that Burgbach was ever an "ausgesprochener Weinort." However, as we have explained, the Weingärtner are still there, though in reduced numbers, and 240 people own Weinberge and many of these work them, at least on a part-time basis. And, too, for every person who works a piece of Weinberg on a steady even though part-time basis, there are usually several others who participate in this work in some way or are directly affected by it. It is also true that about one third of all families in the Burgbach Gemeinde own some agricultural land, including orchard, meadow, and garden pieces, most too small to be commercially profitable. The way of life represented in its fullest form by the traditional Weingärtner-Bauern complex described in Chapter 4 is disappearing, but the relationship to the land in both its rational and nonrational forms is still there, overlaid as it is by all the massive physical, occupational, and attitudinal change that has occurred. To the casual observer, however, these underlying features and patterns are not obvious. Burgbach seems almost wholly converted into its new Glanzzeit.

This change is reflected in the attitudes of Burgbach's young people. The change was clear even as far back as 1960 when thirteen- and fourteen-year-old youngsters were asked to respond to the statement, "The life of a Weingärtner is better than the life of a factory worker. Are you in agreement with this statement or not? Why?" The majority replied as one fourteen-year-old boy did:

> This profession (Weingärtner) is much healthier than that of the factory worker who must work the whole day long by a dirty machine. But in such a business I would receive my pay on a regular basis and also have more free time than a Weingärtner. Therefore, I will chose a job in a factory or business.

Or, as a girl, aged thirteen, said:

> I am for the Weingärtner profession. In the spring, one can work in the fresh air and warm sun on the Weinberge and see how the buds spring up. In summer, it is still more beautiful, when the fresh and green leaves of the vines grow. And in the fall, one can enjoy the big blue grapes . . . but the factory worker has his weekly pay and his evenings free. I shall marry a worker.

Nearly all of the responses indicated a romantic idealization of the work of the Weingärtner in the fresh air and warm sun, and as his own boss. But in the end, the life of the worker in a factory, shop or business establishment wins out because of the practical aspects of regular pay, regular hours, and predictable free time.

These attitudes are a projection of the position of Burgbach as a whole. Burgbach attempts to preserve its idealized identity as a Weinort, while it is well on the way toward becoming an altogether suburban and industrialized community. In the last chapter we will discuss the dynamics of this ambivalence further.

PHYSICAL CHANGE IN BURGBACH

Many physical changes have been brought about in Burgbach as a consequence of its new population and its new internal diversity. The fifty-four new business and industrial establishments built since the war have been scattered throughout Burgbach though concentrated, to some extent, on the Marktplatz, and on former pieces of agricultural land on the periphery of the village. The new factories are all in the *Industriegebiet* (designated industrial area) on the other side of the railroad tracks. Due to good planning, and the dispersion of small establishments within the community area together with concentration of large ones on the periphery in one area, the industrial and business aspect of Burgbach is not as obvious as its residential aspect. New apartment buildings and duplexes do, however, belie the tone set by the ancient Stiftskirche and the remaining traditional *Fachwerkhäuser*. Burgbach is under pressure for the building of more family dwellings. There are 2,085 family units including Ausländer (non-Germans), but there are only 1,516 living units. There is definitely a housing shortage and there has been one ever since the end of the war.[2]

To meet this need, 924 residential units have been built since 1949. These include what we would call both single-family houses and apartments. Each apartment is included as a living unit. These dwellings have added a new quality to the image of Burgbach. They are concentrated in the east, on both sides of the main street, and most recently have been built on sloped land that was formerly Weinberge. In addition, a new development to the west of the town center, now in progress, will include eighty new residences, mostly two-family units.

Despite all the building that has been done, housing tract monotony has been avoided. No group of buildings is so large as to set itself off from the community as a whole. None is so radically different that it jars the image of unity that Burgbach presents.[3] None are so much alike that they become mere replicas of mediocrity.

Another major development has begun between one of the peripheral streets running toward Stuttgart and the world globe factory. In this area there will be a whole new sector, including a shopping center. This project may challenge the physical unity of Burgbach. It will form a strong new focus that will compete with the services and businesses around the Marktplatz. Burgbach, already a Vorort, will have a suburb of its own.

The Marktplatz—the visual, administrative, and shopping center of Burgbach has also undergone dramatic change. The old communal baking house and four Bauernhäuser in the square were demolished and replaced by a very modern Drogerie, a grocery store, and a laundry. But the most important change other than the replacement of old structures and the renovation of others is the new

---

[2] The figure 2,085 includes all kinds of units: man and wife, with and without children; unmarried or divorced man with childen; unmarried or divorced woman with children; and single individuals not incorporated in larger families.

[3] This statement is partially belied by one apartment-house development of several stories but this structure was built in a relatively low area and is consequently not particularly obtrusive.

Newly built apartments against a background of Weinberge where Flurbereinigung has been completed. (Courtesy Don Camp.)

The stream has been canalized and covered over with concrete. It runs under this parking area.

Rathaus complex, together with the very modern post office. Though decidedly modern in its conception and use of materials, the Rathaus was designed to blend architecturally with the ancient Stiftskirche directly across from it. Contained within its complex are the offices of the Town Council, the regional notary, the police, a small library, and the post office.

The development of the Marktplatz required the diversion of the small stream passing through Burgbach which originally ran directly through the Marktplatz area. Today it follows a path that avoids the middle of town and its bed has been deepened and its sides built up in cement and stone. Recently, almost the entire length of the creek, as it runs through the village, has been covered with concrete. Cars are now parked on the newly covered section, but eventually it will be incorporated into a broad street which will pass around the Marktplatz and the central area of the community, thus permitting a faster and safer flow of traffic and at the same time easier access to the town.

Older residents see these changes as destructive of amenities that they previously enjoyed. They point out that now there are not even benches to sit on in the Marktplatz, only places for cars to park. They miss the rose bushes that were planted along the open section of the creek with their profusion of blooms in the spring and summer. Though canalized, there was still water running in the creek that glinted in the sunshine beneath the bending bushes. The old people look out to the margins of an expanding Burgbach and ask themselves how long it will be before there is a solid belt of apartment houses, factories, and shopping centers from Burgbach and beyond, down the Remstal all the way to Stuttgart. The Bürgermeister and his staff are aware of this. They, too, regret some of the consequences of modernization that seem necessary as accommodations to greatly increased population, traffic, and industry. But they regard their job as one of adjusting to the facts of change. They are engaged in planning with other representative bodies from the German government, the Remstal, the Kreis (county) and Land Baden-Württemberg.[4] They project substantial population increases and a corresponding increase in industrialization and urbanization. The possibility of a continuous urban strip along the Rems from Stuttgart to Burgbach and beyond does not seem so remote.

Burgbach seems poised at only the beginning of a dramatic transformation. Will there be any room for the Weinberge, orchards, meadows, and flatland Äcker of grain, root crops, and vegetables? Will there be any Bauernhäuser in the new Burgbach? It does not seem too probable. These are images from the past. They represent nonplanned evolutionary adaptations to the environment and have, as we have explained, certain built-in technological limitations. And yet the complex of man, land, equipment, great houses, and livestock has continued in force right up to the present time in the midst of what looks like overwhelming urbanization. And this complex has long provided satisfactions through its rituals that are not replaced in the urbanization process.

We have pointed out that many of the changes, perhaps all, that have taken place within the old Weingärtner-Bauern complex were substitutive. Elements were exchanged, as in motorization, but changes in principle with potentially transformative consequences did not occur. As a consequence, the old complex continued on, supported, in fact, by the substitutive changes that were made. But now major changes in principle are occurring. Industrialization, conversion to wage work, specialization and diversification of labor, and the material expansion of the urban use of land and space are all major changes in principle, that is, they require nearly total reorganization of the basic relationships among men and between men and resources. One particular process, Flurbereinigung, will be discussed as a clearcut example of a change in principle designed as a rationalization of production. It directly affects the ecological "lock-in" we have described.

Flurbereinigung involves not only the consolidation of holdings by exchange of land titles, so that all of an individual's land will usually be in one area, but also the physical recontouring of the Weinberge themselves. There is usually a long period of negotiating before work starts, since at least 80 percent of the land holders must agree to the process before it can begin. The Bürgermeister of

---

[4] During the past year (1972) there have been intensive discussions about the joining of several communities, including Burgbach, into a larger municipal aggregate. Highways, rapid transit, access to a future freeway, recreational and educational facilities, industry, and land use would all be coordinated within a master plan based upon a population of around 50,000 persons for five communities—an increase of over 100 percent.

A bulldozer goes to work on a sloping piece of Weinberg. (Courtesy Don Camp.)

Burgbach insisted that there should be virtual consensus so the negotiations took longer than they do in some communities. After agreement is reached, work begins. The stone terraces, tool and rest houses, drainage canals, and all other encumbrances are removed, the topsoil is stripped, and the slopes are recontoured. Then the topsoil is replaced and roads rebuilt. The process is most impressive. One stands in awe of man's ability to destroy what has been created through the centuries and reconstruct it in the modern image in a few short weeks. Large earth-moving machines have already reworked the south-facing slopes of Burg-bach's Weinberge. The smooth, unterraced, blank, steep valley sides lie waiting for their new grape vines. They have only a planting of clover and earth-holding grasses on them for the time being. There are no tiny, terraced plots where members of the family can make their hand and back work count. There are no stone or brick shelters, personalized by special decorations and insignia, where tools are kept or one could get out of the rain or cold. Gone are the terraces and drainage channels, built laboriously by hand over a span of generations, often of stones from the castle on the Kappelberg nearby. The very earth itself is different. All the topsoil from all the plots in a given area is mixed together as a result of the Flurbereinigung. The soil of each plot was literally created over the years from compost, manure, eggshells, sand, anything that would enrich and lighten the soil, carried up from the valley below, and mixed with the poor and frequently dense native soil. And it has been kept in place not only by the terraces but also by the back-breaking labor of hauling loads of dirt back up the steep slopes after it had been washed down during heavy rains. Everything is now smooth, contoured, and uniformly impersonal. What are the results of this drastic change?

FLURBEREINIGUNG—A CHANGE IN PRINCIPLE

The antecedent conditions in Burgbach that called Flurbereinigung into being were the same as those existing in other areas of Germany. Most German agricultural land had been split into smaller and smaller parcels. With the shortage of labor which began in the mid-fifties as the "economic miracle" in Germany took place, it became increasingly inefficient to work such parcels. The working of these plots continued in its traditional and ritualized form partly because, with some exceptions, there was no basic intervention constituting a change in principle that would make the development of a new and rational complex of operations possible.

Certain forms of Flurbereinigung have been known for a long time in Germany. Some communities passed laws governing land division and attempted new groupings of existing parcels as far back as 1750. New laws governing the inheritance of land were passed in some areas in 1850, and in the 1930s northern Germany, in particular, was affected by new land consolidation and inheritance laws applied under the Third Reich.

Flurbereinigung must be seen in the larger context of land development plan-

The soil has been enriched for generations by adding manure and compost. These piles must be spread out by hand between the rows of grapevines. (Courtesy Rick Hanson.)

ning carried forward by the federal and county governments and the local community administrations. Comprehensive land and area development plans governing the next twenty-five years are now taking concrete shape. This process began during the Third Reich and was resumed again in 1960 when new federal laws were made uniform and coordinated planning became possible. Planning programs were given impetus by the physical destruction of a large part of urban Germany, the pouring in of millions of refugees, the consequent construction of new housing and the relocation and new development of industrial areas.

One of the major thrusts of the land and area development programs has been the rationalization of German agriculture. During the next few years more than 600,000 farmers must leave the land. Their operations have become economically marginal. This process has already begun. Over 80 percent of the farmers and Weingärtner in Germany have had to supplement their agricultural income with other sources, often by commuting quite long distances.

German agriculture, like folk agriculture in all countries, is heavily ritualized. Every operation, from feeding cows chopped turnips to hoeing weeds in the Weinberge, to tieing prunings from grapevines into identical-sized bundles, is ritualized in some degree. These rituals provide satisfaction, a sense of accomplishment and worth that are unrelated to the goals of production. The rationalization of agriculture calls for the elimination of ritualized practices, the self-subsistence pattern, what we would call the "farming as a way of life" orientation, and conversion to an efficient production-oriented enterprise.

One aspect of the rationalization process is the relocation of agricultural enterprises from within villages to outlying areas. These relocated units (*Aussiedlerhöfe*) represent dramatic deviations from the traditional units of the farmer or Weingärtner in their villages and their relationships to the outlying fragmented plots. The Aussiedlerhöfe themselves are planned for efficiency in layout and are newly constructed. They are rationally related within their integral parts to the enterprise with which the proprietor is engaged, be it hog-raising, vegetable production, or viniculture. Single-product enterprises are favored. An attempt is made to consolidate the land around the residence so that the proprietors of the Aussiedlerhöfe can reach their fields or Weinberge quickly and work it efficiently. It is the intent of the rationalization program that the Bauernhäuser in the inner village should eventually be eliminated. The material advantages of such outlying production units, surrounded by the consolidated land to which the agricultural workers have direct access, are obvious.

The same general principles apply to Flurbereinigung in the Weinberge. Once a Weinberg area has been restructured and consolidated and the new grape vines are producing, the advantages are substantial. There is an increase of approximately 4,600 liters of wine per hectare (2.47 acres), a decrease of approximately .25 D.M. in the production costs of each liter of wine, and a decrease of about 650 hours of work annually per hectare. It is estimated that it takes only about half as much labor to produce about one and a half times more wine. These dramatic production advantages result from specific consequences of Flurbereinigung. In the consolidated and restructured areas there can be a uniform layout of trellises related rationally to the degree of slope and extending consistently over a

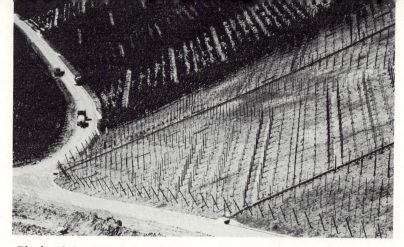

When Flurbereinigung is finished the long, smooth slopes must be replanted. (Courtesy Don Camp.) Compare this picture with the one of the traditional Weinberge on page 70.

large area. This permits the trellises to be laid out sufficiently far apart so that relatively heavy machinery can be used. Mechanization of most operations becomes possible. Flurbereinigung also permits all available frost-free areas to be used and permits the planning of frost barriers and wind breaks in rational relationship to prevailing conditions. The smooth slopes are also all slanted in a consistent direction toward the sun, and since they are unbroken by terraces and uneven surfaces they absorb more heat from the sun. This increases the sugar content of the grapes and a more uniform quality of grapes is produced. It is also possible, as a result of the Flurbereinigung, to rationally match different types of vines to specific soil conditions during the replanting.

The main hardship associated with Flurbereinigung is that the landholder must wait at least three to five years after the process is completed before he can gather a significant harvest of grapes, and despite generous state subsidy, he must pay a substantial portion of the costs of the operation. The loss of income and the added burden of cost is too much for many landholders, mostly those in the small and middle ranges of amount of Weinberg owned. The fully professional Weingärtner are hard hit, but the long-term rewards make the investment worthwhile. Older people, especially those without heirs who will work the land, small owners and hobbyists, and Weingärtner who are marginal producers tend to sell their holdings to larger operators.

The advantages described above are the strong forces for Flurbereinigung. The underlying condition to which it is an adaptation is the shortage of labor caused by the lure of industrial work and wages. This kind of employment in turn was made possible by the adaptation made to the very sudden increase in population right after the war. As the new factories and shops were developed to provide work and consumable products for the new population, many people were attracted from their work on the soil. The extended familial relationships that had been the source of much of the labor necessary to carry along the viniculture operation, done as it was by hand, became unavailable. It became necessary for the work of the professional Weingärtner to be rationalized. He had to be able to do more with less help.

Neither the advantages of Flurbereinigung nor the practical conditions that called it into being overcome the emotional resistance to it. As one woman in her sixties who had worked on the Weinberge all her life and who had inherited three small but productive parcels from her father said, "Where our forefathers painfully labored to build terraces to hold the soil and drainage channels to carry off the water during storms, and where they carried the earth washed down the slope back up again on their backs, now all of that is gone forever. It is painful to see it all destroyed. And what is to keep the soil on the hillside with the terraces gone?"

Without doubt, Flurbereinigung helps the full-time professional Weingärtner who must rationalize their operations if they are to stay in business. But for the part-time cultivators who do not depend upon the Weinberge as a major source of income and particularly for those who are practically hobbyists, Flurbereinigung is of little or no advantage. It was possible for them to go to their postage-stamp-sized parcels on weekends and hours after work and putter around —hoeing, spreading compost, straightening trellises, rebuilding terraces and drainage ditches—and have a real feeling of accomplishment. But as one thirty-five-year-old man with two tiny plots of Weinberg in an area where Flurbereinigung had taken place several years ago said, "I would simply feel foolish going up there and fooling around with a hoe when everybody else is working the land with machinery. It just isn't the same." So he is going to sell these parcels that have been in his family for at least four generations. He will sell them to a landholder who already owns more than five times the size of the average holding of Weinberge.

It is too soon to say just how fast the concentration of land in the hands of a few may proceed in the Burgbach area. Elsewhere in Germany where Flurbereinigung has occurred, this tendency has been marked. *Schwerpunktsbetriebe* (concentrated enterprises) are increasing rapidly as the Nebenberuflichen find the machinery too expensive and the handwork too irrelevant to continue. The principle of concentrated enterprises is, of course, central to the rationalization of agriculture. Similar processes have been taking place lately in the United States as large-scale corporate agricultural operations have replaced the small family farm.

The ultimate outcome of Flurbereinigung appears to be the destruction of the traditional complex of the Weingärtner core culture in Burgbach. The ecological "lock-in" which we have described is no longer functional after Flurbereinigung because the limits placed by small plot size and their distribution are removed. The first fatality will be the Bauernhäuser and the way of life connected with it, including the ritualistic aspects of Weinberg management. A consequential fatality will be some loosening of familial relationships, since these relationships do not have the same economic implications that they do when labor is exchanged, even on a token basis. Consequential to these changes, in turn, there will be changes in basic values, such as love of the land, the ritualistic dedication to work, and the moral value placed upon saving and upon not showing wealth. Perhaps most important, the identity of Burgbach as a Weinort will be blurred. The basis for cultural continuity in many significant areas is reduced or eliminated.

Flurbereinigung, therefore, is not a substitutive change. It is a change in principle which results in a train of consequences that eliminates a whole traditional complex, and the elimination of this traditional complex affects other areas of belief and behavior. We should not, however, overlook the fact that Flurbereinigung does not occur in isolation and cannot be considered a sole cause of the consequential changes we have declared. It can be considered a final cause in a complex of interrelated events and processes. Conversion to a wage economy, industrialization, and the accompanying shortage of labor are prime causes of the conditions that make Flurbereinigung necessary. These in turn were set in motion with greater intensity than would otherwise have been the case by the sudden arrival of a new population with diversified characteristics and needs. Flurbereinigung, though a change in principle and a direct antecedent to the collapse of the traditional, ritualized complex, is in turn a consequence of yet other changes in principle.

In the next chapter we will consider the young people of Burgbach. They are a different kind of generation than has ever appeared during the long history of the village. Most of the young are unrelated to the ritualized complex of activities centering upon the land. They have grown up in a postwar world of economic miracle, technological development, and economic rationalization. They will be the ones who must find solutions to both the immediate and long-range problems that confront Burgbach today. We will consider their schooling, their view of the world, their identities, their instrumental choices, and some of the behaviors in which they engage for which their parents and grandparents have little sympathy.

6 / Schooling and the young people

INTRODUCTION

Cultural systems are maintained through the cultivation of certain attitudes, values, and beliefs in the young, as well as certain skills and knowledge. In complex modern societies this cultivation takes place within the family, in the formal school, in churches, business and industrial establishments, in peer groups, and through mass media. In this chapter we will be mainly concerned with the school, since it is charged with a major responsibility for the maintenance of the cultural system in Western society. Schools in changing communities are also charged with responsibility for mediating change.

Of the various kinds of schools present in the Remstal, we will concentrate on the Grundschule, the basic four-year elementary school to which all German children go irrespective of what educational-occupational route they take after these four years through the Hauptschule, Realschule, or Gymnasium.

The structure of the school system in western Germany seems extremely complicated to the American observer. After four years of Grundschule and at about age ten, children go to one of the above-mentioned three schools.[1] The Hauptschule leads to occupations relatively low in the prestige and income hierarchy and lasts through the ninth year. Most students who graduate from a Hauptschule will also go on to one or another kind of apprenticeship training or vocational education. Children going to the Realschule (or *Mittelschule*) continue through the tenth grade and then usually go on to three years of specialized training in engineering, or to a *Fachschule* or *Berufsfachschule* that gives them advanced vocational training, or in a few cases to a *Wirtschafts-Gymnasium* which stresses economics and business training. The third type of school is the Gymnasium, the "highest" school before the university level, with a curriculum emphasizing natural sciences, ancient languages or modern languages. The professions in their advanced forms are open only to those who have passed the *Abitur*, the final examination given at the end of the thirteenth grade of the Gymnasium, since

---

[1] The structure of the educational system is somewhat different in other parts of Germany. The description applies to Baden-Württemberg.

only individuals who have passed the Abitur are eligible to study at an institution of higher education.

Until recently, these three branches of secondary education have been almost hermetically sealed off from one another. Current attempts are being made to make it possible for children to move from one to another branch by taking special examinations. This attempt has been only partially successful, since each of the branches tends to constitute a self-confirming system in regard to who attends from what economic level and with what cultural and educational background.

A Gymnasium education has recently been made available to more students by the building of more Gymnasien and by encouraging children to enter these schools after finishing the Grundschule. The result has been a considerable increase in attendance at the Gymnasium which has resulted in a further glutting of the higher education facilities of West Germany.

There are other complications in the formal structure of the German educational system, but they are not particularly relevant to our discussion. Our concern is with the elemental processes of cultural maintenance and adaptation, and they take place as far as schooling is concerned mainly in the Grundschule. Further on, however, we will be concerned with the ways in which the Grundschule experience influences the way in which children think about their environment, how it forms their identities and shapes their futures, as they make choices that will affect decisively their styles of life. We will also be interested in the extent to which the Grundschule experience aids in the assimilation of children from divergent cultural backgrounds.

DIE GRUNDSCHULEN

Two Grundschulen will be described. One is in Burgbach, and the other is in nearby Schönhausen. These two villages are different from each other in that Schönhausen is in its own little valley connecting to the Remstal, whereas Burgbach is more centrally located in the Remstal itself. Their locations have affected the pace of urbanization. Burgbach has expanded more rapidly and is today more than twice as large as Schönhausen. Burgbach also looks more modern and is losing its Fachwerkhäuser, replacing them with modern apartment houses or business establishments. It has already undergone a radical renovation of its central area, and planning for the future is based upon the assumption that Burgbach will become at least a town and join with other population nuclei in the immediate area of the Remstal, as a part of an organized metropolitan area. Schönhausen will always be a little bit off to the side and may be able to preserve more of the amenities of semirural life that now are so apparent. Nevertheless, Schönhausen too, has been caught up in the urbanization process. Its population has doubled since World War II; its brook has also been canalized and covered over with asphalt. Some of its beautiful old Fachwerkhäuser are likewise being replaced by more crass commercial structures, even on its main street. And as in

In Schönhausen the traditional Fachwerkhäuser predominate.

Burgbach, only a small minority of the people still work the land and live in Bauernhäuser with their livestock and farming equipment. Most of the people in Schönhausen, as in Burgbach, work in factories or business establishments, and about half of them commute to work.

The two communities have much in common, not only because they stem from the same local culture and have the same ecological orientation, but also because they are urbanizing and industrializing. Though their outward appearances are quite different, the Grundschulen are alike in many respects, and the children are sent to the same advanced schools in the immediate area.

The Burgbach school sits well above the Marktplatz. Down the gently sloping hill below it are several old Bauernhäuser. Across the street is the village cemetery. Modern duplexes, apartment buildings, and some single-family dwellings have been built on the slope above the school. The view from the Grundschule is truly beautiful, looking out across the ancient Stiftskirche, over the roofs of the old part of Burgbach to the Weinberge on the hills rising from the other side of the Remstal.

On the Marktplatz side of the school there is a black-top playing area about 50 by 120 feet, completely without recreation equipment or even painted lines for different games. The recesses there are almost wholly unorganized, since all equipment is located in the *Gymnastikraum*, a recreation hall nearby. All games

played during the recess period are, therefore, individual or group efforts requiring considerable imagination as well as gross physical activity. There is always
jumping, skipping, hopping, wrestling, piggy-backing, tag, and racing. Often a
guessing game is played where two people tangle up their arms and legs in very
complicated patterns, with the guesser trying to figure out how to undo them—
lifting a leg over an arm, here, unwrapping a leg from a neck, there. Another
game uses a giant rubber band stretched between the legs of two children in a
changing pattern, manipulated by children at each end of the band, while the
players attempt to jump in and out of it without touching it.

On the wall by the front door of the very modern schoolhouse in Burgbach is a
giant mosaic, extremely modern in style and message, presenting a man and
woman very close to each other and distinguishable only by hair length, with fish,
animals and landscape, and the rising sun in the background casting its rays over
them. Inside, the walls of the hall offer samples of each class's art, often quite
unusual to the perception of the American visitor. On the wall by the stairway
leading up to the main floor, certain sayings are framed: "Serve everyone in
reaching the best of his capabilities," and "He who does not regard God as the
truth does not believe in his fellow man."

Upstairs, the long hall is split into two levels. Entering any classroom one is
first struck by the large windows in the far side of the room. They reveal much of
Burgbach, including the Stiftskirche, as well as a large section of the Remstal and
the vineyard-covered slopes and forested ridges on the valley side across from the
school. The view from the classroom itself seems to be a constant reinforcement
of much that goes on within the classroom.

The Schönhausen Grundschule is much older, built at the turn of the century,
in the ponderous German public-building style of that period. It is surrounded by
a cemented and asphalted area which, in front, serves as a parking lot for
teachers' cars, and along the sides, as a playground. As in the Burgbach Grundschule, there is no play equipment and children play the same self-created games
or simply run about during the short recesses. In back of the school there is a
large area composed of about equal parts of garden and turf maintained by an
Oberlehrer (senior teacher) and his family who live in the back part of the school
building.

As one enters the Schönhausen school, one is reminded immediately of the old
style grade schools in middle-western towns in America with their creaking
wooden floors, rooms that are either too hot or too cold, windows set in massive
walls above eye level, and walls distinguished by brown stained and varnished
wood and more-or-less cream colored plaster, with light globes suspended from
the ceilings. Children's drawings enliven the walls here and there, as do an
occasional natural science exhibit or map, but the overall impression is rather
drab.

Directly adjacent to the school is the Schönhausen church which is much older
and very distinguished in appearance. Within it are the beautiful fourteenth and
fifteenth century frescos that were uncovered and restored in the recent renovation of the church. In the tower, that part of the church closest to the school, are

four massive bells that ring periodically and are heard very clearly in the classrooms. Across from the school and up the street as far as the eye can reach are Fachwerkhäuser, and down the street is the Rathaus, built in the fourteenth century and carefully maintained into the present. The children in the Schönhausen Grundschule cannot escape the visual and sensory impact of tradition. Nor as they walk down the street or look out of the windows of the school can they escape the impression, given the vineyard-covered slopes totally surrounding Schönhausen, that this village is still a Weinort. The traffic down the street in front of the school, the new and very modernistic post office, the new bank being built in a place vacated by a Bauernhaus, the modern building for gymnastics and other indoor sports, the public swimming pool, and the new factories springing up in the flatter land in the valley below Schönhausen (as the valley opens into the Remstal) also remind the children that things are changing.

In the Classrooms: Burgbach School

In the third-grade class in the Burgbach Grundschule, Herr Gauss, a pleasant man of about forty, is teaching *Rechnen* (arithmetic), "Frau Sweet cooks six pounds of raspberry jelly, twelve pounds of apricot jelly and eight pounds of strawberry. She fills two-pound glasses. How many glasses does she need?" Herr Gauss conducts a continual question-and-answer session, using all possible variations of the problem. The children are so excited that they are chattering, jumping out of their seats, hands are waving frantically, some are shaking their fingers so vigorously that their joints crackle. Their excitement seems unlimited and unrestrained as they try desperately to be recognized. They cannot tolerate a wrong answer by one of their peers, and groan desperately when one makes a mistake. When the noise level gets too high, Herr Gauss says somewhat sardonically: "I am happy that you are so loud. It makes a good impression. Very good. . . ." But he says it gently.

After Rechnen comes *Singen* (singing). The children begin singing a song that they have learned already. Three girls practice on wooden recorders. After the song is played once through, the whole class sings it with the accompaniment of the recorders. Then a new song is introduced. One child reads it, then all recite it after him, then all sing together. There are several parts in the song.

(*Chorus*): A grain sifter comes down the green path, wearing a colored coat, and bows before Liese.
(*Boys only*): Maiden, my beautiful maiden, shall we dance a little?
(*Girls only*): I wouldn't like to dance, thank you, I am waiting for a king.
(*Chorus*): Then comes a merchant's son down the green path, wearing a jerkin of silk, and he bows before Liese. Later comes a little tailor down the green path, wearing a green coat, and he bows before Liese. But Liese waits year after year beside the green path, and not a single king comes, and no one speaks to her.
(*One boy sings*): Maiden, maiden, beautiful maiden mine, shall we dance a little?
(*One girl sings*): Oh, how nice dancing would be, were it only with a king.

(*Chorus*): Finally comes a swineherder, Jochen Christoph Stoffel. He has neither shoes nor socks and wears only wooden slippers, and Stoffel dances with her, the proud Liese.

In this song, as in most of the stories that are read later during *Lesen* (reading) periods, there is a moral. The proud Liese gets her comeuppance. The story that is read in Lesen, which comes next, is a reversal of the theme of the song about Liese. It is a Grimm fairy tale written in script. The story is about a bear which turns out to be none other than the prince. Two boys are not paying very much attention to the story. They are being *böse* (bad) and so Herr Gauss quietly tells a girl to write five Zs (*Zeilen*, or lines to be written) after the boys' names on the side blackboard. Mostly boys' names appear on the board, a notable exception being one girl, Angelika, who must just naturally be böse, since her name appears on the board so frequently.

After a short recess in which a great deal of explosive physical self-expression takes place in the playground, the children return for *Naturwissenschaft* (natural science). Herr Gauss is explaining the water cycle and draws a well-organized and very expressive diagram on the board showing rain falling on the valley slopes from the clouds above, the sun and its hot rays, the evaporation process, and the rain falling to earth again. He goes on to talk about the importance of water, both in the biological cycle and for human needs, and ends with items of local interest. "The Schnait Creek flows into the Rems, the Rems flows into the Neckar, the Neckar flows into the Rhein, and the Rhein flows into the sea." He uses a combination of lecture and question-answer method. He brings one child up to the front of the classroom and asks her this question. "Where will the water run down faster—in the vineyard or in the forest?" He promises, rather dramatically, to show the children something very interesting if they are quiet, and leaves the room. Returning with a jar of soil in his hand, he tells the story of a great rain with water running down the Weinberge much faster than in the forest. As though he were revealing a great secret, he explains that the pound of dirt in the jar came from only six liters of water running off the Weinberge. He explains how the Weingärtner has had to pack the dirt back up the slope in wooden carriers. The children have seen such carriers, either in the Heimat Museum or among their families' own equipment. Herr Gauss talks about how important it is to keep plant cover on the slopes and what functions the forest on the ridges serves. As he talks, he points out the window where both the Weinberge and the forest can be seen.

The next day Herr Gauss begins his class by calling on a child to read today's paragraph-long story. This story had been assigned to the class several days before. The children were supposed to write a rough draft of the ending of the story for the present class and then write the final copy into their notebooks during the last part of the class, after they had discussed various possible endings for the story: "Die Strasse ist kein Spielplatz" (the street is not a playground).

The mother had said very often to her Walter, "The street is not a playground." But whenever Walter's friends came to him after school, he had forgotten it again. On a beautiful afternoon the children played soccer in the street. The ball rolled again . . . a man on a motor scooter. . . .

Herr Gauss begins asking questions about what might happen. A boy states the expected general possibility. "He can crash." A girl suggests that the scooter driver cannot brake quickly enough so that Walter is run over. Another child, upon Herr Gauss' prompting, adds the next step: "Someone quickly telephones the police." And Herr Gauss says, "And what do the police do then?" He receives no satisfactory answer from his pupils so he says: "They take a picture of the accident scene." The story moves on, dark and predictably getting darker. Walter is put on a stretcher. A girl is called upon to write the word "stretcher" on the board and she misspells it (*"Tragbane"* rather than *Tragbahre*). Herr Gauss says quickly: "Das ist falsch," and another pupil goes to the board to write it correctly. Once inside the ambulance, Walter is taken very quickly to the hospital. Asked to describe what happened a boy says Walter's *Fuss* (literally "foot") was broken. "Nur die Schwaben sagen das (only the Swabians say that)," says Herr Gauss, going on to explain that he meant the entire leg, or "Bein," and the Swabians say "Fuss" when they mean the entire "Bein." His response is not atypical for teachers not born in Swabia. They regard learning to speak High German as highly desirable, since it is likely that many of the children will not spend their entire lives in Swabia. They tend, however, to go sometimes a bit further and give the impression that Schwäbisch is a lower form of speech.

Herr Gauss announces that enough possibilities have been explored, and the pupils take out their *Aufsatz Hefte* (essay noteboks) and begin writing their final copy. The handwriting is well rounded and clear. Many of the themes in the children's essay notebooks are concerned with being careful and with the bad consequences if they are not.

Heimatkunde

The next subject this morning is *Heimatkunde* (local history and culture). Herr Gauss draws an *Ortsplan* (village layout) on the board, showing new houses and commercial buildings, the new Rathaus, trees, the Marktplatz, and marked areas to be developed. The children copy down every detail of what he draws and says, using colored pencils to mark off different sections of the Ortsplan. Herr Gauss teaches a lesson about town planning and incorporates with it instruction on linear perspective in drawing. The Heimatkunde notebook into which the children place this lesson and others, is titled, "Warum wir Heimatkunde treiben" (Why we study Heimatkunde).

Heimatkunde is: exploring and getting to know our homeland. We want to get to know our hometown next and its surroundings in Kreis Waiblingen. In particular, we will look at the streets, houses, places, people, fields, meadows, mountains and valleys, and animals and plants.

A diagram, somewhat enigmatic from the American observer's point of view, follows.

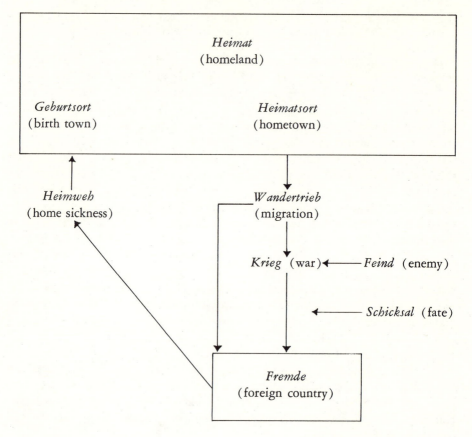

Following in the Heimatkunde notebook are these major subject divisions.

I. *Mein Vaterhaus* (my family home). The front and side views, presumably of their own family home, are carefully drawn and colored in by the children.

II. *Unsere heimatliche Heimat* (our native homeland). Under this heading there is a description of the geography of the area and its location in Greater Germany and in Europe.

III. *Der Tageslauf der Sonne* (daily journey of the sun). Under this heading there is a diagram showing the sun rising and setting, connected by arrows from the ocean with a sailing ship drawn on it. On the land there is what appears to be a replica of the Stiftskirche. Above the land and Stiftskirche there are the horizon and the sky.

IV. *Die Windrose*. Here, the four cardinal directions and the bisecting axis are drawn and labelled appropriately with the various towns in the Remstal area related to these points of the compass.

V. *Von Wind und Wetter* (of wind and weather). Wind direction and the wind strength at different times of the year and the meaning this has for growing things, for activities in the area, and for human moods and feelings.

VI. *Unser Kirbemarkt* (our harvest market). "Once in a year in the spring on a Thursday is the harvest market in Burgbach. The selling stands are built in the market square and up the next street. Already on Wednesday evening the boards are stacked in preparation, and the area for the stands is divided off.

Early Thursday morning came the manufacturers and shopkeepers of Burgbach and many neighboring towns with their cars and set up their stands and wares. At the market there are stands with sweets, sports equipment, hot weiners, clothes, shoes, hats and caps, domestic wares, and so on. In addition, there is the cattle and livestock market with suckling pigs, swine, and calves. At the wood market, there are boards, posts, bean poles and posts for the Weinberge."[2]

VII. *Die Weinlese* (wine grape harvest). Here, with descriptions and drawings, the children cover the wine-making process including the work of the Weingärtner in the Weinberge, the harvest techniques, and methods of wine making. The pictures include a pitcher, shears, a grape-harvest basket, and a bunch of grapes. Why there are red and white wines is also explained and some of the different kinds of grapes that make different kinds of wines are described.

VIII. *Die Wind oder Wetterfahne* (the wind or weather flag). *Ostwind*: clear, dry weather, in summer hot, and in winter cold. *West-Südwest und Nordwestwind*: this means rain in the summer and snow in the winter. *Südwind*: this means usually warm weather in the spring, and ice and snow in the winter. *Nordwind*: in the winter this brings great cold.

IX. *Die Tiere als Wetter Propheten* (the animals as weather prophets). "When the swallows fly low, there will be rain soon."

"If the frog climbs out of the jar, there will be good weather."

"If he sits there, rain will come."

"When dogs and cats eat grass, so say the people, 'there will be bad weather.'"

And various other topics.

X. *Unser Friedhof*. The location of the Burgbach Cemetery is mentioned, the graveyard is described, and some of the birth and death dates are indicated.

XI. *Unsere Kirche*. This section includes a considerable essay on the history of the Stiftskirche and drawings of it from its major perspective and from both sides.

XII. *Der Kalender*. How the year is divided up in the calendar, the different lengths of the months and what they are called.

XIII. *Jahreszeiten* (seasons of the year, festivals, etc.). This section covers all the cyclical occurences in Burgbach and the Remstal, mentioning all of the religious holidays as well as the secular festivals such as Fasching and the Kirbefest.

XIV. *Ortsplan*. This is the current topic and includes a topographical description of the village, its major sections, planned renovations and the planned additions by way of commercial, industrial, and residential development.

The general plan of the Heimatkunde curriculum followed in Burgbach was also covered in the Schönhausen Grundschule, although with somewhat different content related specifically to Schönhausen. Both emphasize the local scene and contextualize this scene in the Remstal, in Kreis Waiblingen, and Land Baden-Württemberg.

The Schönhausen School

In both Burgbach and Schönhausen, classroom learning is frequently supplemented by expeditions (*Wanderungen*) outside of the classroom. One long hike taken by Herr Steinhardt's fourth-grade class in the Schönhausen Grundschule

---

[2] This description is idealized, and paints a picture of the market much more relevant to prewar days than the present.

and one short trip to the bell tower of the Schönhausen church will be described, drawing from the author's field notes.[3]

Die Wanderung

Today I went on a Wanderung with Herr Steinhardt's fourth-grade class. We left at 8.05 A.M. and returned at 2.35 P.M., having walked in a circle route from Schönhausen, along the ridge of the valley and back. We walked almost entirely on small paths through forest, Weinberg, and meadow, for nearly 18 kilometers (about 11 miles). The purpose of this expedition was very general, as described to the class—to observe firsthand the geography, plants, animals, and economy of the area, and to see some local historical sites; in short, anything of interest.

We walked at a brisk clip all day, with short breaks for a snack, and then lunch, and brief stops to examine things of interest. The children showed no fatigue. At the end of the day they were still talking excitedly and jumping into any intriguing place they found along the way. The American professor was not as fresh, though Oberlehrer Steinhardt seemed just fine. I cannot imagine a fourth-grade class in the United States that would be able, much less willing, to make this hike.

The children had a high degree of freedom. They walked in their own groups, sometimes at a considerable distance from the main body, or alone, which a few did. They climbed to what seemed to me to be dangerous heights, especially on a tower overlooking the valley that we visited, and crossed highways and roads on their own. The teacher said that although he would be legally responsible for an accident, he did not feel there was any point to the expedition if the children were too tightly controlled. He had spent considerable time, however, in his classroom preparation for the trip explaining to the children what the hazards were and the extent of his responsibility. When one or two of the boys did something really dangerous, he called sharply to them, and they desisted immediately.

The freedom extended to personal relations among the children, and in certain ways, to their relations to the teacher. He was called from every side, constantly, and usually in a contraction of his name to something like "Herrhardt." Children, especially girls, walked in twos and threes with him, and frequently with one holding his hand on each side. The handholders took turns. I was offered the same treatment after awhile.

The instructional values of the walk were obtained without explicit effort. When we came across a small pond with frogs and salamanders in various stages of metamorphosis, specimens were caught and retained in bottles for later observation, and the teacher reviewed their growth cycle, which had been gone over in detail in Naturkunde, in the classroom. Several species of trees were identified and reference made to their growth characteristics, their distribution, and their economic uses. This material was also familiar to the children from classroom work and reading. When we climbed the tower overlooking the Remstal, the teacher pointed out each of the communities in the valley below, their relation to the waterways, and to the city, visible in the distance. He commented on the very apparent zones of forest, Weinberg, and flat garden land, and on the new apartment buildings and industries plainly identifiable in the valley. The children had examined in detail a map of the area in Erdkunde lessons, and had learned in the class all of the things the teacher talked about.

[3] The Schönhausen study was done during the spring and summer of 1968, with subsequent visits in 1970 and 1971. The work was supported by N.S.F. Grant #GS2106 and the Faculty Research Fund, School of Education, Stanford University. It is reported, in fuller detail, in *Education and Cultural Process*, edited by G. Spindler (1973).

Their interest, as they peered about from the very top of the tower, which was about 100 feet high and on the crest of the ridge above the valley, was acute. One had the feeling that the images of map and actuality were vividly super-imposed. They asked many excited questions about things they could see spread out below them. For most this was the first visit to the tower, even though they lived in what Americans would regard as the immediate vicinity. The parents of more than half of the children were not born in the Remstal. Herr Steinhardt said that parents rarely took their children on local expeditions, though many went fairly far afield on annual vacations to Spain, Italy, the North Sea, and so on. In families that did not take trips free time was usually spent visiting relatives. He felt that the real value of the Wanderung was to "just explore the local area, and to do something interesting together."

When we came to a large open meadow circled by forest not far from the tower it was almost filled by a vast flock of sheep. Though the area was bisected by two small, black-topped roads and there was considerable traffic, one man and two very busy dogs kept the entire flock under control. The children walked through the flock. One or two minor indiscretions by adventurous boys were brought sharply under control by the teacher. We stopped to talk with the shepherd, a somewhat unsocial man who spoke very thick dialect but answered questions from the teacher effectively enough. He spoke (insofar as I could understand him) about how the flock was controlled, where the dogs came from and who trained them, when the sheep were sheared, and the problem of disease.

Schwäbisch was spoken by all of the children (including offspring of Zugezogenen) when they spoke with each other. When they addressed me they used Hochdeutsch, though sometimes they responded to questions from the teacher in Schwäbisch. The bilingualism did not seem to cause any distress. It was taken for granted; not an issue.[4]

The Trip to the Bell Tower

The teacher is a very gifted, expressive, talkative, intelligent, older woman. She is a regional historian, has written a definitive history of Schönhausen, and writes poetry with a special flair. She captures the attention of her class with stories drawn from her own experience, or from chronicles that she has studied. She leaps about, sings, changes voices, plays her violin, gestures, acts out, imitates animals and sounds made by bells, whistles, and screeching wheels, to illustrate her points. I have never been so entertained and intrigued by any public or private performance anywhere, as I was almost every time I visited her classroom. She also shook my stereotypes about German schoolrooms by grouping the children at tables in work and talking groups. Her classroom is among the noisiest I have visited in Germany or the United States, except when she is performing. The children move about with apparently complete freedom, and talk to one another incessantly, even when the teacher is shouting instructions about the lesson they are doing from the front (or the middle) of the room. I asked her if the noise did not bother her and she said, "Yes, sometimes, but children must talk to learn. Their talking is positive (*positiv schwätzen*). When it is not, I stop them from talking." Indeed, most of the talking I heard was positive—concerned with the

---

[4] Joshua Fishman and Erika Lueders-Salmon have compared the teaching of high-German to dialect-speaking children to the teaching of "standard" English to speakers of "Black" English in a provocative paper on the sociology of language (1971).

task, or at least not disruptive of it. And the children produced well—in lessons accomplished, in group performances of skits and acting out of dramatized lessons, in music hour participation (with singing, triangles, cymbals, recorders, a xylophone, rhythm sticks, and hand-clapping), and in art products, such as crayon drawings and water paintings of impressive complexity and style drawn of the center of Schönhausen, as one might see it on a medieval map. Again, from the author's field notes.

This morning the lesson is about the history of the four great bells in the tower of the church in Schönhausen which is near the school. The teacher shows pictures of the tower and the bell at various periods of history. She draws the four bells, each of which has a different history, on the board, and identifies the parts. She describes each bell in detail; exactly when they were cast, when melted down for armaments, when and by whom recast, and what tones they produce. She gives this history without pathos. The children seem impressed by the fact that the bells have served for both war and peace, and that the form of something may stay the same even though its constituting materials change completely. The teacher then explains, with some expressiveness, why the bells ring, and how these functions have changed over time, and change now, as they did then, over the seasons: to awaken people, to tell them to go to bed, to call to vespers, to announce weddings, to give notice of invading armies and as a call to arms. She gives vivid details on how the church and the community made different demands upon its members and citizens in late medieval times, and during the late nineteenth century, in contrast to the present, and how these demands are reflected in the times and ways the bells ring. The bells are the voice of the community in both its sacred and secular dimensions. The children "oooh" and "aaaaah" during the presentation. Some of this response seems a little "put on" to me, but after talking with the children about it I decided that this was my projection. The teacher ends the classroom lesson with a song with a "ding-dong" theme. She plays it once on the recorder, then sings it, then has the children sing it with the recorder accompanying.

Then we all get up and walk over to the church tower, a short distance away. We climb up the several flights of rough wooden stairs (actually almost ladders) covered with pigeon leavings, to the loft where the bells are. The last ten feet are especially difficult to negotiate, so the teacher goes first (she is near retirement!), then helps each child up through the narrow opening at the top of the "stairway." The bells are enormous, each weighing more than a ton, suspended on huge beams, and run by a very sturdy, but electrically powered and timed mechanism. Each bell is identified and the children are reminded of things the teacher has said about them. While we are still in the loft the mechanism begins to whirr and clank, and the bells start ringing. The noise is total. The children cover their ears and shriek, both of which are probably good protection against deafness. The teacher laughs (while holding her ears). She planned it that way. We all leave the loft. None of us will ever forget our visit to see (and hear) the bells of the evangelische Kirche in Schönhausen. I believe that the children will also remember what Frau Müller tried to teach them about the history of the community and the role of the bells.

Comment

Each of these learning experiences was successful, on the terms presented by the teachers, and they all communicated specific content as well as generalized attitudes about the history of the area, about Schönhausen itself, and in the first expedition, about nature and man's relation to nature. The principle of integrated learning was always evident—the teachers planned each lesson to teach more than one thing at a time—and the emphasis was on the local area, places the children could see, and experience directly. These appear to be precisely the kind of learning experiences that should lead to a commitment to the local cultural system in its more tradition-oriented than urbanized form. Nevertheless there are also many dimensions to these experiences (the observation of the spreading urbanization and industrialization of the Remstal visible from the tower; the discussion of the changing functions of the bells and the community needs, etc.) that prepared the children for instrumental choices that move well beyond a traditional frame of reference, even though some form of identity relevant to Schönhausen is retained. Identities are being reinforced, while specific knowledge and attitudes are being acquired. The locus of the identities is the local community, its history and its immediate area, but this locus is not an absolute. It seems transferable and enlargeable.

Criticism and Revision

Revision of the elementary curriculum, textbooks and other materials, and presumably of educational philosophy is at present underway, stemming mainly from the centralized administration of schooling in Baden-Württemberg and prompted by increasing consensus on the part of professional intellectuals and some politicians that the German educational system is antiquated. The Heimatkunde curriculum is an object of special concern in this revision. Many German educators have felt that the emphasis upon local geography, history, and culture is inappropriate to the expanding participation of German citizens in the modern world and that in some ways it smacks of the land, folk, and blood pattern of the Hitler period. Many of the older teachers, particularly those from Swabia, resent this change. They point out that many of the higher officials in the Ministry of Education are not Schwäbisch themselves and have little interest in or regard for the local area and its history. The older teachers feel that children should start by learning about things familiar to them, that they themselves can see and experience, that they can learn better about the outside world if they have learned about the immediate world to which they can more easily relate. We will touch upon this controversy later and apply some research results to it.

Whatever controversies there may be about Heimatkunde or whatever changes may have occurred or be occurring, at the time that we studied the Burgbach and Schönhausen schools, Heimatkunde, Naturkunde, and Erdkunde were taught in the style that we are describing. It is appropriate that we should concentrate upon this style, since it was the one that the adults of the populations of Burgbach and Schönhausen themselves experienced as children, and one that their own children in turn have experienced. We think this educational experience has had a significant influence on the course of events in the Remstal villages as urbanization has taken place. Heimatkunde and its associated emphases in related subject areas, we hypothesize, has provided a common identity for children in the heterogeneous Remstal communities, though the commitment to this identity may not run very deep for many children. This orientation may act, in later years, as a constraint on the ability of children to make an adjustment to the urban scene. For the moment this is an open question. However, Heimatkunde is certainly not all that is taught in the Grundschule, and within the framework of Heimatkunde, the urbanizing environment is taken into consideration.

Materials of Instruction

Besides classroom and extra-classroom experiences, one must consider the materials of instruction if the purpose is to describe the school as a culture-transmitting process. Examples of all the various categories of the published books, manuals, lesson guides, etc., used by the teachers in the Schönhausen School were collected. Most of the same books and manuals are used in the Burgbach School. Following are examples from two textbooks, both for the third school year and both "reading books" (*Lesebücher*). The first is one published in 1957, *Haus in der Heimat*, and used in 1968 when the study was done. The other, *Schwarz auf Weis*, was published in 1967, and was still being used in 1971. It should be noted that neither of these books are directly associated with either Heimatkunde or Naturkunde; they are prepared for the teaching of reading.

A selection from the 1957 book, titled "Frühling in der Grosstadt" (Spring in the big city, p. 5), is paraphrased below:

In the middle of the great city, among tall, gray houses, the autos, streetcars, and people, stood a woman with a basket of spring blossoms. They had only this morning come in from the country on the early train and they were very lonesome. In the country the sky is so wide and blue, the air so fresh, and the earth so wonderfully green. One hears nothing there but singing birds, the brook, and now and then a murmur from the village. One sees only the sky, the forest, the paths, and the garden with its many, many colorful blooms.
"I am dizzy, and I've got dust in my eyes," said the violet and sank her head.
"And not a butterfly is there to see or to fly over my yellow dress the Narcissus complained.
The bushroses were not satisfied either, "Here there is no wind to flutter our white skirts," they said.

The story goes on, each of the flowers with a specific complaint directed at conditions in the great city. The woman keeps trying to sell the flowers, but everyone hurries past, intent upon their business. Only a little girl stops. A bouquet would make her mother happy, so she chooses some of the blossoms that would please her the most and takes them home.

Oh! how happy the little flowers were, as they stood on the table, explaining about the forests and meadows, the stars and the sky. They described everything so beautifully that everyone in the room believed they sat outside in the lovely spring. Instead, they sat in the huge city.

The book contains fairy tales, little stories, poems, descriptions of nature, short essays on the garden, the first *Maikäfer* (a plant-eating beetle that occupies a special place in the literature of the Grundschule), the zoo, the fire station, annual seasons, and ceremonies. Frequently presented themes include:

Personification of plants and animals.

Magical events, people, places, animals.

Nature, land, garden, village, are clean, friendly, fun, and warm; the city is the converse of these.

God protects us all. He made everything beautiful, particularly nature.

Mother and father take care of us and ask nothing in return.

There is a secret, wonderful world of childhood where adult realities need not intrude.

In general there is considerable sentimentality centering upon mother love, home, God, comrades, animals, and plants, and the beauties of the country, nature, and gardens. There is only one story set in the city "Die Stadt erwacht" ("The city awakens"), and one poem about the railroad station. The book is beautifully illustrated with tasteful, imaginative watercolor paintings.

The orientation of reading books for the lower grades has been the subject of commentary by German educationists and social scientists. As concluded in *Das Bild der Heimat im Schullesebuch* (Ehni 1967:241), "The Heimat as the essence of cultivated feelings, of the internalization of the world, and of retrospective sentimentality has become questionable, and is no longer useful as a pedagogical goal." But this conclusion is modified to the effect that values the Heimat orientation was designed to communicate should not be overlooked (by implication) in the reorganization of schoolbooks and curriculum. It is the heavy sentimentality and the unreality to which there are objections, and the 1957 reading book is really a mild example.

In fairness to the teachers of Heimatkunde, Naturkunde, and Erdkunde at the Schönhausen and Burgbach schools, it must be emphasized that the total range of lessons and experiences covering these subjects moves far beyond the rather heavy sentimentality of some of the readings. When Herr Steinhardt demonstrates the geography, demography, and ecology of the Remstal by taking his pupils to the top of a tower overlooking the valley and points out things they have already learned about in the classroom, he is not merely perpetuating the picture of the Heimat represented in school reading books. When Frau Müller takes the children to see the bells in the church and contextualizes this event in a solid presentation of local history and a functional analysis of the community and its demands upon its members she is not merely transmitting sentimentality. She (and Herr Steinhardt) use *sentiment* to communicate the content of the lesson units, as all educators must, if children are to accept the credibility of the content.

The current movement against Heimatkunde and its associations may destroy or seriously weaken the implicit values of this subject matter and the learning process associated with it. This could have unfortunate consequences, since the configuration that has been described may have been a significant factor in the development of a common identity among children from diverse backgrounds. This may, in turn, have been influential in the assimilation of the great influx of new population, and in the relatively smooth ongoing transition from an essentially folk community to an essentially urban way of life.

A Changing Curriculum

The changes in the curriculum and teaching methods following upon recent educational reforms have only begun to be an influence in Burgbach and Schönhausen schooling at the Grundschule level.[5] We may pick up some clues as to their probable direction by looking briefly at a story from one of the new reading books, *Schwarz auf Weiss* (1967). Though published in 1967, this book was not used until the fall of 1968 in either of the communities. The scene is China (paraphrased from p. 10).

> Little Pear stands by the river that goes past his village. His mother has told him to be very careful and not fall in. But he does, just as a houseboat, with a family, including three children, goes past. He almost drowns, but is saved. They go downstream to the next dock, perhaps a mile or two. Little Pear talks to the children while they drift along. They ask him about his village, family, fields, animals, etc. All their lives they have been on the boat. He gets out at the dock, finally, and runs and runs toward his village and home. He is so glad to see it in the distance, and even happier when he is embraced by his mother, father, grandparents, and siblings.

Perhaps the change in emphasis between the old and new reading books is not so great as it at first seems. The village and its associations (family, fields, animals) are still presented in desirable terms. But as one Schönhausen teacher said, "Why do we have to start with strange and far-off places? Why can't the children be taught to value their own surroundings first, and then be led to an understanding of the rest of the world?" Indeed, the educational theory standing behind Heimatkunde is familiar to American elementary school teachers—it is sometimes called the "concentric ring" theory—that experience should begin with the familiar and widen out to the unknown. *Schwarz auf Weiss*, however, appears to have changed the scene, but not, in this story, the theme. The consequences of this are indeed difficult to foresee, but one sympathizes with the teachers who know their local area well, and who regard it as a resource in the transmission of a unified view of reality.

However, to be fair to the "new wave" it must be pointed out that *Schwarz auf Weiss* is less heavily sentimental, there is less emphasis on the small village and cosy valley, less personification of plants and animals, fewer explicit moral lessons, and more straightforward descriptions of places and events. The locale shifts about from China to Italy, to Siberia, to India, to Eskimoland, and often to generalized Germanic locales. There are also some classic fairy tales, thirty-five poems (of which eighteen are about nature or animals). And there are some very flat-footed descriptions of events, such as the abrupt death of a migrant worker in the city who tries to cross a busy street against a red light and is run down, that

[5] We remind those readers familiar with German that we are not following case endings in the use of German words in the context of English sentences. The endings are dropped in order to avoid confusing the reader who does not know German.

would probably not be included in a third-grade reading book in the United States. The reading books for the third grade described in this chapter seem more advanced than comparable materials from American schools. The sentences are long and complicated, the vocabulary large, the ideas quite sophisticated, the illustrations superb, and the material is very imaginative.

It seems probable that there will be a shift in emphasis in the Grundschule, but that there will be enough continuity so that the major conclusions of the study reported in this chapter will remain viable for that part of the Remstal represented by Schönhausen, and for some time, even Burgbach, though the area itself becomes *de facto* urbanized.

Freedom and Constraint in the Classroom

All of the classrooms visited in the Schönhausen school were closer to the "free" end on a continuum of explicit freedom and constraint. If one were looking for support for the authoritarian hypothesis in these classrooms one would be frustrated. Some of the classrooms verged on bedlam, but I never saw a classroom out of control. In general, the more experienced and secure the teacher, the freer his or her classroom. It was only the younger and relatively inexperienced teachers who attempted to keep the classroom quiet much of the time, irrespective of whether or not this quiet was necessary, or even relevant to the learning process presumed to be taking place.

If I had visited the freer classrooms only a few times, I would have left quite puzzled, for I would not have understood how order could ever be maintained, or how any kind of intervention for control could ever take place. As Herr Steinhardt said, "This school is not based upon fear, it is based upon love. Children do not learn well when they are anxious. They must feel free." This is precisely the philosophy I have heard enunciated by leading personnel of "free" schools in the United States, including one in which I played a role for several years. And at first that is the way it seemed to be in the Schönhausen school. But there is a difference.

One day while I was standing outside the door of the school at the dismissal of the classes, a line of fourth graders rushed past one of the senior teachers, in their usual hurry to get outdoors. The teacher smiled as usual, but there was something in his look. Suddenly he reached out to cuff a boy on the side of the head as he went past. The boy barely flinched, though it was a goodly cuff, and continued out the door, his face set and somewhat reddened. I was astounded, and as soon as I could, asked the teacher what that was all about. The teacher said, "That boy knew what I would do. He sat in class for the past hour pestering the girl sitting in front of him. I suggested he stop it, but he chose not to do so. I don't like to make issues of such things during class time, so I punished him as he left the school." I watched the boy carefully after this incident for overt signs of resentment against the teacher or the school. I saw none. Nor did I see any change in the teacher's behavior toward him. It was apparently a normal incident. The punishment was abrupt, direct, and was, it seems, considered deserved.

With this experience behind me I began to look more closely at the problem of freedom and constraint. I observed numerous incidents that could be described as "the use of force." One of the younger but experienced teachers called without warning, as far as I could see, a rather large boy up from the back to the front of the room and gave him a resounding whack on the face with her open palm as soon as he arrived. He stiffened, set his expression, and returned to his seat without a word. My attention was diverted from him after awhile. Again without warning, the act was repeated. I again inquired of the teacher. "He was playing around. He hasn't done any real work for three weeks." I asked why she hit him the second time. "He didn't get back to work." I talked with the boy. He was laconic, but said, in effect, "Fräulein Scherdt is ok. I like her. I should work harder." The punishment did not appear to have the meaning of chagrin, embarrassment, personal degradation, that I was projecting as I viewed the incidents. But no one really enjoys an *Ohrfeige* (box on the ear).[6] They are avoided. The threat of one is always present, but it is a simple, direct threat. I do not believe that the children in these classrooms became neurotic in their fears; if the same happened in American classrooms they might, for the cultural meaning of such punishments would be quite different. In any event, the teacher would be in deep trouble in many communities.

Other techniques are used that can be described as "patterned warning interventions." For example, when classes really threaten to almost break the windows with their shouting and shuffling about, the teacher may suddenly command attention, and have the children sit down quietly. Then suddenly the teacher shouts "stand up," then "sit down," then up and down several times, including a few "remain seated," or "remain standing." In this way the teacher reestablishes his or her command. The noise level quickly goes back up, but the children are reminded that the teacher is ultimately in charge and that limits do exist.

The limits of behavior are known, and the punishments for exceeding them are usually predictable. Within those limits a wide range of behaviors are tolerated by teachers. The situation in schools elsewhere in Germany doubtless varies. We have some data on other classrooms in nearby schools, and something of the same balance of freedom and constraint seems to obtain, though some of the classrooms are more strictly controlled than was the rule in the Schönhausen school. In the Burgbach school the classes were somewhat more tightly controlled than in Schönhausen, but none of those observed could be described as heavily authoritarian. Rebhausen (Warren 1967) is somewhat similar though, again, the classrooms there seem more constrained than in Schönhausen.

I have not, of course, described all the mechanisms of constraint. The teachers tend, for example, to lay out tasks very carefully, and with considerable emphasis on the right order. When pictures are drawn they are drawn of certain subject matter, and criteria having largely to do with representation of reality are applied. When themes are written they are written in a certain hand, with certain spacing. Children are expected to accomplish tasks at their own speed, with freedom to move about, ask questions, make small innovations, but the task is defined for

[6] See Warren (1967) for the use of *Ohrfeige* in Rebhausen.

them and the criteria applied to them are the teacher's. The teacher does not let go of the class at any time, even though to the foreign observer it may seem at first that most teachers have no control at all over what the children are doing. When any lesson is being worked out by children at their desks, whether in free discussion groups, or individually, the teacher is walking about, examining the work, commenting on progress, sometimes placing a hand, with a certain amount of pressure, on a child's head to direct his or her attention to the task, or lightly tapping the child's hand or head. These touches seem almost like caresses, and they are very light, but the distance between this kind of caress and an Ohrfeige is not as great as one might think.

But the combination of freedom and constraint seems very effective. The children have the security of knowing what they are supposed to be doing, and of how far they can go in deviant behavior. Within these known limits the authority figures are benificent, responsive, very human . . . and they are good communicators of information and skills.

Identity and Choice

It seems clear that schooling at the basic elementary level in Burgbach and Schönhausen provides children with a means for forming an identity related to the village and its local area. The question we are left with for the Remstal children is whether, given this identity and its localization, children are able to expand their frame of reference sufficiently as they grow up to make relevant choices in an increasingly urbanized environment. The question for children in the United States is almost the reverse. American elementary schools in communities of roughly comparable economic standing, with their elaborate teaching aids, stress on the relationship of learning problems and teaching procedures to individuals, general richness of material educational environment, as well as in the organization of the curriculum itself, seem to be oriented toward a complex, internally differentiated, open, urbanized society. But it is difficult to see how American school children can achieve any sort of identity within this experience. With what can they identify? The supermarket (usually a part of the social studies curriculum)?[7] The profit motive? Capitalism? Set theory (the new math.)? With the teacher? With the Eskimos (a part of the social studies curriculum in some elementary schools)? Perhaps a clearcut identity would be inappropriate, even dysfunctional in United States society, and yet the lack of one is lamented by youth, teachers, and intellectuals.

The intended identity in the two German schools we have described is clear, and curriculum content and teaching methods are appropriate to it. The present constituency of Burgbach and Schönhausen is from many different parts of Germany and its former outlying populations, and is diverse in religious, linguistic and regional cultural background. Do these two schools provide common identity for children from this diverse population?

[7] See Durkin *et al.* (1964).

INSTRUMENTAL PERCEPTIONS AND CHOICES

We can now consider the effects of the Grundschule experience more precisely. These are our questions: does this experience place limits on the recognition and choosing of alternatives in later life related to the urban society? Does this experience provide the basis for the assimilation of divergent populations to a common cultural standard? What evidence is there of identity formation, and if so, what is it? Some of our research was directed specifically at these questions. As a part of the research strategy, we adapted the Instrumental Activities Inventory developed by the Spindlers for research on other sites, and applied it in both the Grundschulen and in more advanced schools. The technique as developed for research in Germany consisted of a total of thirty-seven line drawings of thirty-seven activities that are instrumental to the attainment of goals considered appropriate in the Remstal area. Activities instrumental in the traditional as well as the urbanizing, industrializing Remstal are included. The technique is designed to elicit from respondents their preferences for certain instrumental activities and goals and their rationale for these preferences. The activities are not only occupations such as working in a factory, being a chemist, or being a Weingärtner, but also such things as having a dinner for friends at home, or going to a lively party in a public place of entertainment, going to church, living in a particular kind of house, going to school, and commuting to work. The goals are to be thought of not only as specific attainments such as a certain income or possession of a certain object, but as life styles or conditions of being which may subsume a number of specific preferences and instrumental activity-goal linkages. Rather than being a personality test, the Instrumental Activities Inventory (I.A.I.) is a technique for eliciting responses relevant to the perception of social reality and the alternative possibilities contained within it (Spindler and Spindler 1965).

Every research technique should be related to a theoretical model. We use a model of a cultural system upon which we must expand a little. It is possible to understand the results obtained by using the I.A.I. at one level, without understanding the theoretical model. A statement of it is included for those whose interests extend beyond the data relevant to this particular case study. The statements following are applicable to all complete cultural systems.

A THEORETICAL MODEL

A cultural system operates so long as acceptable behaviors usually produce anticipatable and desired results, and unacceptable behaviors usually produce anticipatable and undesired results. These behaviors can be thought of as *instrumental activities*, and the results as goals, or satisfactions. Beliefs that are part of the cultural tradition support the accepted relationships between activities and satisfactions. The relationships are *credible*. The credibility of the instrumental relationships is an essential attribute of the system and one that schooling is designed to support. Both goals and the activities instrumental to them are socially sanctioned. These sanctions may not involve a consensus of all the members of a cultural system, for various subgroups, classes, and cliques within the whole system have their own goals, instrumental activities, and sanctions. The relationship between given activities and the goals or end-states to which they are instrumental may be thought of as *instrumental linkages*. Activities may also become goals in themselves in that they may become so satisfying that the original goal to which they are linked becomes of secondary importance. The linkages are dynamic. *Social control* may be defined as sanctioned intervention in the operation of the instrumental linkages for members of a cultural system, by other members. *Social organization* is the organization of personnel and their roles in relation to each other, and of the necessary materiel, so that the linkages can function. Education as *cultural transmission* may be defined as means employed by established members of the cultural system to inform new members coming into the system of the sanctioned instrumental linkages, to communicate how they are ranked, integrated, and in general, organized, and also to commit these new members to the support and continuance of these linkages and the belief system that gives them credibility. (In this sense educational institutions serve mainly functions of reaffirmation and recruitment.) The *cognitive structure* in individual minds that results from this education consists partly of this organization and related commitments, insofar as cognitive structure is relevant to perceived social reality. *Cognitive control* as socially relevant is the ability of an individual to maintain a working model, in his mind, of relevant and at least potentially productive instrumental linkages and their organization. When I.A.I. data are analyzed, we will refer to *supporting values*. Supporting values are situations, events, or states of being that are used by respondents to justify expressed instrumental preferences. All acceptable activities and end-products have "value," but some have more than others. Unacceptable or negatively sanctioned activities and goals may be said to have "negative value." *Identity* may be defined as individual commitment, often at an ideal level, to a given configuration of instrumental linkages and supporting values, and to symbols representing them. This commitment is at least partly verbalizable.

This system model is open-ended and provides for adaptive change. During rapid culture change established instrumental linkages are challenged by new information and behavior models. Their credibility is weakened. Their operational viability declines. Alternative linkages are recognized, acquire credibility, and become operable. The range of alternative instrumental linkages from which individuals may choose increases. The total range will include a number that conflict. Cognitive control becomes more difficult.[8] In studies of culture change one may be concerned with either the culture system processes (economic, technological, political) that result in new instrumental linkages, or with the perception, selection, and cognitive ordering of alternative linkages by individuals.

[8] Attempts to maintain cognitive control under conditions of radical cultural confrontation may result in expulsion of conflicting instrumental linkages, reaffirmation of some, synthesis of selected elements, or segmentalized adaptation. See G. Spindler (1968) for some relevant theoretical background.

THE RESEARCH PROCEDURE

We can now convert our questions to the frame of reference described above. We want to find out whether children from different backgrounds choose the same, or different, instrumental activities, anticipate the same ends, and rationalize their choices similarly (or differently). We want to identify the influence of the school on these choices, and, particularly, in the ways the school may act as a constraint upon urban-oriented instrumental perceptions and choices. We are also interested in changes that occur as children mature, and in sex differences. And we want to discover whether there is a common identity fostered by the school experience.

Though we could, and did, use all thirty-seven I.A.I. drawings in individual administrations, it was necessary to select a smaller number for administration to classroom groups. After we had administered thirty interviews on an individual basis and used the line drawings in their original form with one Gymnasium class, we selected seventeen, for which we had 35 mm. slides made. These seventeen were selected as particularly diagnostic of different orientations with respect to the process of urbanization, "folk" to urban, and as relevant to our particular sample. By using two 35 mm. slide projectors simultaneously, we were able to show in classrooms seven pairs of pictures from which children were asked to make choices as well as three pictures shown singly that they were asked to evaluate. A simple data sheet filled out by each child included such items as birth date, father's occupation, birth place, birth place of parent, etc., as well as two essay questions.

The drawings (see pp.122–131) include a contrast between the traditional Fachwerkhaus and a modern single-family dwelling; a Weingärtner versus a white-collar office worker; factory workers versus an independent owner of a small shop; a farmer and family working on a flatland plot versus a machinist working at a lathe; the Grundschule with children going into it; a traditional church as compared to a rectangular, very modernistic church; a large-scale farmer with his helper working with a very large tractor plow versus a technical draftsman; a large and modern Bauernhaus with stalls for stock, lofts for hay, machinery, etc., combined with a family home; a dinner table with party-style settings but clearly in the home, versus a very lively party in a public place; the grape harvest showing a wagon and several people, including children, pouring grapes into it.

These drawings were shown with two 35 mm. projectors to 282 children in the Grundschule in Schönhausen and in a nearby Hauptschule which is attended by children from both Schönhausen and Burgbach. They were also shown, in the same manner, to the teachers in the Schönhausen Grundschule and to a sample of 31 parents of children attending this school. As stated, the technique was also administered, using somewhat different procedures, to one Gymnasium class and to 30 individuals representing various schools in the area. Besides the responses elicited by pictures, we asked for short essays stating agreement or disagreement with two statements, one supportive of city as against village life, and one supportive of being a Weingärtner as against being a factory worker. The essay questions were included to elicit global, generalized orientations toward rural-village versus city life, rather than responses to specific instrumental linkages relevant to village versus city life. The details of the results are presented elsewhere (Spindler 1973), and we will summarize only the most relevant parts.[9]

THE RESULTS

In the essay responses the children in the sample as a whole show an idealistic bias toward life in the small village. These responses are not differentiated by regional, linguistic, religious background, urbanization, or origin of parents. There is a common outlook. Specific values offered in support of village life include: fresh air; less traffic; quietness; nearness to nature; friendliness; and availability of fresh foods. City life is seen as: noisy and dangerous; there is no place to play or walk; the air is bad; life is impersonal.

The same general bias operates in the essay responses in favor of the life of the Weingärtner, without significant variation as related to any background factors excepting sex and age. Supporting values for the Weingärtner life style include: self-determination and independence; being near nature; breathing fresh air; having healthier work; being owner of one's land.

These choices of Weingärtner and village are supported at a highly idealized level. The configuration of choice and supporting values seems to be virtually a replication of what children are taught in school in the Heimatkunde lessons. The bias is persistent at the older grade level, although there are significant statistical differences between older and younger children, and also between girls and boys. Girls tend to be more urban-oriented in most of their responses than the boys, and older children more than the younger.

The teachers in the Schönhausen Grundschule, from whom responses to the essay questions and the I.A.I. were also collected, share these idealized biases toward the Weingärtner-village way of life. They are consistent, too, in the supporting values with which they rationalize their choices. The parents are like the teachers.

However, when the specifics of pragmatic choice are presented to the children in the form of the paired instrumental activities expressed by I.A.I. pictures, the children tend, with certain exceptions that will be noted, to choose in an urbanized direction. For instance, when they are asked to choose between a traditional Fachwerkhaus and a very modern single-family dwelling, they choose the modern dwelling more often. And they support their choices with such values as: convenience; luxuries; practicality; a better life; more comfortable; easier to keep up; warmer; more valuable. Girls tend to choose the modern house more frequently than the boys and there is a tendency for the younger children to prefer the traditional house.

When presented with a choice between white-collar office work and Weingärt-

[9] The sample of 282 pupil respondents was computer programmed for every conceivable combination of urban-rural, regional, occupational, sex and age factors, and statistical tests run in distribution of I.A.I. responses in relation to these differences. I am grateful to Erika Lueders-Salmon for her help on this and other aspects of the data analysis.

Traditional Fachwerkhaus

Modern single-family house

White-collar office worker

Weingärtner

Factory workers

Independent small shop operator

Farmer   *Machine worker*

ner, white-collar office work is preferred. Specific values supporting the white-collar positions are: regular hours of work and free time; more regular pay; cleaner work; not such hard work; more pay per hour; and independence from the weather. Younger children choose Weingärtner more frequently, and girls choose white-collar work more frequently. In both instances, the teachers are more tradition-oriented than the children in their choices, choosing most frequently the traditional house and the Weingärtner occupation.

In the choice between being a factory worker or the independent owner of a small shop of some sort, more of the children prefer the latter. Supporting values include: being one's own boss; making better money; owning one's own shop and equipment; being surrounded by less noise; and having fewer people to deal with. Independence of rules, hours, and goals set by others was the most frequently cited value. But again, girls preferred factory work more frequently because of its security and regularity.

In choosing between farmer and machine worker, there was a moderate preference among the children for the latter. Parents and teachers were strongly divergent ʿrom the children, choosing farmer much more frequently. The children supported the choices of *Maschinenarbeiter* with: secure and regular job and pay, physically easier work and cleaner work.

When shown the picture of the school and asked to express their liking or dislike for it, most of the children liked it, and parents and teachers agreed. Supporting values for school include: specific subjects and teachers that were especially enjoyed; the necessity of schooling for the future; and just plain "like it." Many responses were qualified in what we have come to regard as the typical

School

"Swabian" way: "almost all, but not all, go gladly"; "many are enthusiastic, some not." Older children tend to dislike school more frequently.

Between the old and the new church, the majority of the children prefer the old church. Parents and teachers are consistent with them. Supporting values include references to age, history, tradition, and beauty.

Between the large-scale farmer and the technical draftsman, the majority of the children in all grades choose the latter. Supporting values for the draftsman cited by children include: good pay; pleasant kind of work; independence of weather; clean work; not such hard physical labor (as the farmer); evenings free; regular vacations. The teachers choose the farmer.

When shown the picture of the modern Bauernhaus and asked whether they would like to live in it, a bare majority of the children (51 percent) said they would. They supported their choice with: lots of space; modern; better for children to live near animals; outdoor space; interesting things going on; would like to work as a farmer; living in fresh air; living in the village or out in the country.

When asked to choose between a party at home versus a party in a public place, the children tended to choose the affair at home, but there was a clear difference between the older and younger respondents, with the former choosing more frequently the party outside of the home. Girls choose the party outside more frequently at all ages. Supporting values for the affair at home include: quieter; more control over what happens; less expensive; more gemütlich; family-oriented; and not so wild.

The last picture, that of the grape harvest, was supported very strongly by all grade levels. Values evoked in support of enthusiasm for the grape harvest include: it is just fun; one can eat grapes; it's a good kind of work; one can enjoy the nice, early fall weather and be out in the sun; one can be with friends and relations; one can be out in nature.

In all choices, not just those where teacher choices were mentioned above, teachers tend to be more village and tradition-oriented than the children. Parents are more like the teachers than their children are, but are less conservative than teachers. And the children's responses are significantly differentiated by age and sex, but not by regional origin or any other background factors. Younger children choose village-land-nature more frequently than do older ones, and girls make urban-oriented choices more frequently than do boys.

INTERPRETATION

The choices with which respondents are faced in the essay questions do not require finite pragmatic judgments of an instrumental nature. Respondents express their generalized, idealized, value orientations. The pattern of responses to these two statements suggests a sentimental identification with the village and its associated supporting values.

But what is the depth of this identity? The responses to the I.A.I. pictures do

Old Church   *New Church*

Large-scale farmer

Technical draftsman

Bauernhaus

not seem to be constrained by it.[10] Pragmatic considerations become important when respondents are faced with finite instrumental choices. The village-land-nature identity therefore may be regarded as idealized, perhaps even, in a sense, as "spurious," in that it is not possible to apply it consistently to the real choices presented in an urbanizing environment.

That this idealized identity is consistent with the emphases in the school curriculum, teaching materials, classroom and outside of classroom experience, and the teachers' explicit biases does not prove that the Schönhausen school produced it. The majority of the parents also share this identity, despite diverse origins. School and home are consistent with each other, so far as our present sample of parents indicates and insofar as we are concerned with the idealized identity configuration. They both apparently transmit the same messages. Perhaps parents who live in small villages like them, or must believe they do. Or perhaps only people who like village life stay there. These are variables that we have no way of controlling with the scope of our data at present. But the fact remains, the school appears to transmit an idealized identity and supporting values that are oriented in a certain way. The children appear to have accepted these values and this identity at one level of cognitive organization.

However, when the children are faced with finite choices, during the presenta-

---

[10] One of the more interesting writings on identity processes is by Treinen (1965), whose research indicates that identification with a given place is the consequence of membership (at some time) in a social system that is closely bound to that place, and that is symbolized by place-names capable of eliciting complex emotional reactions—feelings of "identity," or place-reference. Something of this kind may be operating in the identification by respondents of themselves as "villagers" even though they express various urban-oriented instrumental preferences.

tion of I.A.I. pictures, that force them to express a preference for a more village-nature-land or a more urban-linked instrumentality, they tend to choose the latter, though the proportion doing so varies by age and to some extent by sex. The majority prefer modern apartment houses to live in, white-collar office work, working as a machinist, or as a technical draftsman, to alternatives that are clearly village and land oriented. The supporting values for these choices are very pragmatic: better pay, more security, regular hours, independence of the caprices of nature, guaranteed vacations, cleaner and less physically exhausting work.

Party at home

Party in a public place

Grape harvest

When "romantic" instrumentalities, uncomplicated by pragmatic realities, are presented to the children—the old versus the new church, and the Weinlese—the majority express preferences in a traditional, village, land-oriented direction—the beautiful old church and enthusiastic interest in the grape harvest. Possibly the school is also supported as a part of this configuration. These choices do not challenge pragmatic orientation and are a logical extension of the idealized identity revealed in preferences for small village life and the Weingärtner occupation expressed in the essay responses. This identity survives where it does not conflict with practical considerations.

The cognitive organization of the majority of children in our sample, insofar as relevant to our research problem, is therefore comprised of three parts: (1) the idealized identity—villager and Weingärtner, with supporting values: independence, quiet, friendliness, love of nature, etc.; (2) the pragmatic instrumental preference system (modern house, white-collar work, etc.), together with supporting values such as regular income and hours, security, less hardship, etc.; and (3) the romanticized, nonpragmatic instrumental preferences (traditional church, Weinlese, village life) and their supporting values such as beauty, freedom, health, etc. The majority of the children appear to maintain cognitive control over these three potentially conflicting dimensions, perhaps because pragmatism has priority in critical areas of choice. Also, a compromise is, in reality, possible since one can live in a small village, and commute to a nearby city to work.

The interpretations stated above are given general support by the fact that the older children closer to full instrumental participation in society tend to choose more pragmatically, and consequently are more urban oriented. Conversely, the younger children are more frequently village-land-nature oriented in their choices.

As the time of entry into the adult instrumental structure nears, the choices become of greater pragmatic significance.

It is of considerable interest that the teachers definitely, and the parents somewhat less so, are more oriented toward village-land-nature, and are more "romantic" in their view, than are the children, particularly the older ones. The teachers are not faced with the necessity of making the same practical instrumental choices as the older children. They can allow the idealized identity that is present somewhere in the responses of almost everyone in the sample to dominate their cognitive organization. The fact that the children seem capable of making pragmatic choices that are divergent from those of their teachers (and often their parents), particularly as they grow older, suggests that the school as a culture transmitting agency does not act as a powerful constraint. Possibly the Heimat and Natur lessons in the Schönhausen school are broad and realistic enough to provide means by which children can come to grips with the practicalities of life in the urbanizing Remstal.

It is important that the children's responses are differentiated by age and sex, but not by the regional origin of parents, or even by the size of population aggregate (city, town, or village) in which the parents (or child if from outside Schönhausen) were born. Although we cannot prove decisively that the school assimilates this population of diverse background (about one half of the school population is derived from a recently immigrant, Zugezogenen population) to a common standard, the probability that it has some significant influence in this direction seems high. The Grundschule has apparently acted both as a stabilizer of culture and as a mediator of a changing culture.

The school helps provide an idealized identity that is not a barrier to full participation in a changing cultural system. This identity may serve useful functions. If identity is as significant as many social scientists claim, then the result has been positive. A common framework of communication is created and sustained for a diverse population. That the identity is, in the absolutely practical sense, spurious, is unimportant. Keeping a village-land-nature identity intact in the midst of an expanding urban complex may have helped the Remstal avoid the disasters that seem inevitable in analagous situations in the United States. Most importantly for the future, the children educated in the Grundschulen do not seem to have been crippled by this identity. Though they idealize village and land, they can make instrumental choices, and provide relevant support for them, that are oriented toward the urbanized future of the Remstal. They have already moved beyond their teachers and parents in their understanding of the contemporary world, but share with them some significant aspects of a common identity.

THE DEVIANTS

Not all the children of either native or migrant parents in the Remstal grow up with a conflict-free village-oriented identity, "spurious" or not. The situation as we have described it is most relevant to the two villages, Burgbach and Schönhausen, that we have studied. Our description should be more or less adequate for other communities of comparable size, equidistant from urban centers and with the same ecological orientation. It is less applicable to youth in more urban centers, and changes are taking place everywhere.

An increasing number of young people in the Remstal area dress in clothing that seen through adult eyes has a "hippie" aura. Some dress in "mod" fashion. Many boys effect long hair, though more Gymnasium students wear their hair longer than do students in other schools. A few engage in demonstrations against the Establishment, or openly reject their parents and their way of life.

There is also a drug subculture developing. There is a high degree of communication within what we can call a "hard core" aggregate (see Chapter 2) of drug users. "Hash" (hashish), similar to American "pot," or "grass" (marijuana) but probably more predictable in its effects due to impurities frequently found in marijuana as it is purveyed in the American market, is universal. These youths also experiment with "acid" (L.S.D.), mescaline, heroin, "speed" (amphetamines), cocaine, and various commercial drugs. This hard core aggregate offers various forms of aid and support to its participants, including offers of places to sleep, food, and psychic reinforcement. Within it attitudes of antagonism to all forms of adult authority and scorn for established norms of conduct governing sexual behavior are held in common. And of course the drug experience and the sharing and purveying of drugs are an important part of the life style. In general, the way of life, the shared identity, within this aggregate of hard-core drug users is a direct confrontation with the basic values and identities of the einheimisch Remstal culture.

The basic supporting ideology of the hard core aggregate is confrontation and dropout. The participants in this hard core seem to express the same ennui and disenchantment with modern society as does the proportionately larger group of young people in the United States. Some of these attitudes, in milder form, appear to be developing in a wider population of the young in the Remstal. They may increase in intensity and extent as the urbanization of the Remstal increases, though there is nothing inevitable about this relationship.

What is probably more important for the future of the Remstal is that most of the young are opting for a way of life and for instrumental opportunities that were not available to their parents. Weingärtner complain that their sons are not interested in "taking over the land." Young people complain that there is "nothing to do" in the smaller communities, and increasing numbers opt for a more urbanized environment. The idealized, romanticized values centering on land and village do not govern instrumental choices for them.

CONCLUSION

We have studied the Burgbach and Schönhausen Grundschulen and their influence upon children who, as young adults, must make character-defining choices of occupations and life styles in an urbanizing environment. Those schools must serve the same general purposes as do similar institutions in urbanizing America. The Remstal schools provide the basis for communication between children from culturally divergent groups, and their assimilation into a shared cultural framework of meanings and values. This sharing of a common identification with village, land, nature, and folk in the earlier years of childhood and in the form of romantic idealization in later years does not appear to inhibit a wide and pragmatic range of adaptations relevant to an urbanizing environment.

An until now divergent subculture of drugs, relaxed sexual mores, and confrontation is developing among Remstal youth. It may not expand to the proportions that similar subcultures have in the urban portions of the United States, but it is symptomatic of some of the same underlying conditions. The credibility of the established instrumental linkages and old identities is being eroded by radical changes in the conditions of existence. That some aspects of the old culture and identity have persisted, is an indication of the strength of the family and basic school as socializing institutions, and the forces for continuity that we described in Chapter 4.

Spurious identities, though useful in providing some common ground for diverse elements, are unlikely to serve for long when the cultural system and the conditions of its existence are undergoing transformative change. Burgbach and Schönhausen are just entering the age of transformation. What new images that will guide commitment and shape behavior will emerge? Perhaps none will, and the Remstal will decline into the state of goallessness and low morale that often accompanies rapid urbanization, industrialization, and rationalization where the credibility of established identities is decisively challenged. On the other hand, the combination of romanticism and pragmatism that is deeply characteristic of the Swabian world view and the interaction of natives and newcomers in the dynamic Remstal population seem likely to produce new and viable identities and supporting values. It also seems probable that although these identities and values will be a sharp departure from the old ones, they will exhibit some continuity with the past.

TO COME

Whatever continuity of identities there may be, the changes taking place during the decade to come will transform the Remstal from a still recognizable landscape of small communities, farmland, vineyard, and forest to a great metropolitan area. Freeways will cut ruthlessly through forest-covered ridges. Population will increase to more than twice its present size. Consolidated municipal governments will replace separate administrations, including Burgbach's. Community identities will be blurred. Already the marks of individuality and tradition upon the Weinberge have been obliterated by Flurbereinigung. The relationship of man and animals to land is already drastically altered.

The new cultural system with its rationalized technology is very different from that which has persisted for so long. It is different in principle. It consumes air, water, and other precious resources and replaces little. It groups and moves people in anonymous relationships. It is less constrictive, more exciting, and less reassuring. It may also be less enduring than its predecessors. We will continue to observe it. Perhaps there will be a sequel to this case study, a product of collaboration between Stanford students and the anthropologist.

Glossary

Abitur: Final examination after the *Gymnasium*.
Äcker: Farmland; used in this study with reference to small plots in the valley.
Akademiker: University graduate.
Angestellte: White-collar workers.
Apfelmost: Cider.
Apfelsaft: Sweet cider.
Apotheke: Pharmacy where prescription drugs may be obtained.
Arbeiter: Semiskilled and unskilled workers.
arm: Poor.
Aufsatzheft: Essay notebook.
ausgesprochen: Emphatically or decidedly.
Backhaus: Communal bakehouse.
Bauer: Peasant, today also indicating farmer.
bäuerlich: Rural or rustic.
Bauernhaus: The large several-storied structure housing livestock, equipment, and
    people.
Beamter: Civil servant.
Berufsfachschule: School for specialized vocational training.
Berufsschule: School which every apprentice to a trade has to attend.
Bettdampfbad: Being wrapped in damp towels or sheets while in bed.
Blut: Blood.
böse: Naughty.
Brav: Good.
Bürgermeister: mayor.
Deutsche Mark (DM): Unit of currency evaluated at approximately 31 cents
    in West Germany (1972).
Drogerie: "Drugstore" which is not allowed to sell prescription drugs.
Drogist: An individual who manages a *Drogerie*.
einheimisch: Native, but not necessarily Schwäbisch.
evangelisch: Protestant.
ewig: Eternal.
Fachschule: School for specialized vocational training.
Fachwerkhaus: A house with wooden structural beams showing.
Fasching: Carnival at the end of winter before Lent.
Federdecke: A feather-filled comforter with a removable cover.
Fest: A fiesta or fair, a celebration.
Flöte: Recorder, like a small, simple flute.
Flüchtling: Refugee, one who fled, usually from East Germany.
Flurbereinigung: Farmland consolidation in both physical and legal dimensions.
    When applied to vineyard consolidation it is technically *Rebflurbereinigung*.
Frau: Woman; not necessarily "wife" (*Gattin*) but any mature female.
Freiherr: Freeman.
Fremde: Foreign country.
Friedhof: Cemetery.

Frühling: Spring.
Fürst: Prince, sovereign.
Fuss: Foot.
Galgenhumor: Gallows humor.
Gastarbeiter: Guest workers.
Gasthaus: Tavern with rooms for overnight guests.
Geburtsort: Birth town.
Gemeinde: Community, including the agricultural area.
Gemeinderat: Town council.
Gemütlichkeit: Geniality, sociability, coziness, comfort.
Genossenschaft: Association.
Glanzzeit: "Brilliant time," or "golden age."
Graf: Earl or count.
Grosshändler: Big businessmen.
Grosstadt: A large urban city.
Grundschule: The elementary school extending through the fourth grade only.
Gymnasium: A secondary school leading to the *Abitur* and the university and
    therefore mostly to professional occupations.
Handwerker: Skilled workers.
hauptberuflich: Having a job as a main occupation.
Hauptberuflicher: Someone who has a certain job as a main occupation. We
    would usually refer to such a person as a "professional."
Hauptschule: The school from which the majority of children graduate at the
    age of fifteen. It does not lead to profesional work as a rule.
Haushelferin: Household helper.
Heilkraut: Medicinal herb.
Heimat: Homeland.
Heimatfest: A celebration connected with the homeland or the community.
Heimatkunde: Classes or subject matter specifically concerned with the local
    area, its history and ecology.
heimatlich: Native, or homeland oriented.
Heimatort: Hometown.
Heimweh: Home sickness; considered a real illness by some.
Hochdeutsch: High German.
Industriegebiet: An industrial area, usually set aside in a *Gemeinde*.
Industriegemeinde: A community with a heavy concentration of industry.
Jahreszeit: Any particular season of the year.
Land: Land, or a political-cultural area like Baden-Württemberg.
leer: Empty.
Lesen: Reading.
lustig: Gay and jolly.
Kaiser: Emperor.
Kalender: Calendar.
Kaufleute: Sales personnel or small businessmen.
Kellerei: Wine cellar or cellarage.
Kelter: In Swabia it is the central building where grapes are collected and pre-
    pared for processing.
Kenner: Someone who knows (is knowledgeable about something).
Kirbe; Kirbefest: Wine-harvest festival with many nonharvest elements.
Kirche: Church.
Kolrabi: A kind of turnip.
Kräuter: Medicinal herbs.
Kräutertee: Tea from medicinal herbs.
Kreis: County area.
Krieg: War.

Kuchen: Any of various forms of coffee cakes typically made from sweet yeast dough and often topped with fresh fruit and whipped cream.
Magen: Stomach.
Maikäfer: May beetle, cockchafer.
Markt: Market.
Marktmeister: The man responsible for the market.
Marktordnung: The rules for the market.
Marktplatz: The marketplace.
Marktstrasse: Market Street.
Maschinenarbeiter: Machinist.
Meister: Master.
Mist: Manure, usually piled in a boxlike concrete structure about 10 by 10 feet square.
Mittelschule (Realschule):   The school that in level of academic demands ranks between the *Hauptschule* and the *Gymnasium*.
modern: Modern.
Most: "Hard" cider.
Musikverein: A club that sponsors and furthers musical interests.
Naturkunde: Lessons concerned with nature, biology, and ecology.
Naturwissenschaft: Natural science.
nebenberuflich: Part-time, not done as a main occupation.
Nebeneruflicher: A part-time worker.
Nerven: Nerves.
neuapostolisch: New Apostolic.
Norden: North.
Oberlehrer: Master or senior teacher.
Ohrfeige: Box on the ear, a slap; usually actually administered to the cheek.
Ort: Village, place, location (*Dorf* is literally "village").
Ortsplan: Village layout, showing streets, buildings, fields, etc.
Osten: East.
Platz: Place, space (as in *Marktplatz*).
Rathaus: Town hall.
Rationalisierung: Process of rationalization.
Realschule   (see *Mittelschule*)
Rechnen: Arithmetic.
Reibebad: Vigorous rubbing of the body with wet and dry towels.
Reich: Empire, realm.
Saft: Juice, preserved in cans and bottles, and made from a wide variety of fruits.
Salzkuchen: A "cake," similar to white bread but salty and crunchier.
Sauerkraut: Pickled shredded cabbage.
Schicksal: Fate.
Schwabe: A Swabian.
schwäbisch: Swabian.
schwätzen: Dialect expression for talking.
Schwerpunktsbetriebe: Concentrated enterprises in a given area.
schwerfällig: Dull, slow, cumbersome.
Singen: Singing.
Sitzbad: Bathing sitting in a bathtub with water up to the waist.
Sonne: Sun.
Sportverein: Sports club.
Stahlmöbelfabrik: A factory producing steel furniture.
Stammtisch: A table in the tavern reserved for a regular group.
Stiftskirche: A *Stift* is an endowment or grant of lands and property for a church as well as a papal permission to found a church and hold services (*Kirche*- church).

Student: Student.

Süden: South.

Tee: Tea. (Teesorten: kinds of tea.)

Tageslauf: Daily routine or course.

Technische Berufe: Technical professions.

Tier: Animal.

unbeweglich: Inflexible, unbending, fixed, unresponsive.

Verein: Association or club, usually centering on some interest such as music or sports.

Vertriebener: A banished or exiled person, cast out from his or her homeland.

Volk: Folk, the ordinary people.

Volksheilkunde: Traditional medicine used by the people in a society. Folk healing art.

Vorort: A suburb, usually a village in the vicinity of a large city in which commuters live.

Wandertrieb: The urge to migrate.

Wanderung: An excursion.

Wechselbad: Bathing in alternately hot and cold water.

Wein: Wine.

Weinberg (plural, *Weinberge*):   Vineyard, but used in this book to denote small, usually hilly pieces of grape-growing land, technically properly denoted by the next two terms.

Weinbergshang: Slope with vineyard on it.

Weinbergsstück: Plot of vineyard.

Weingärtner: One who is a skilled cultivator of grapes used for making wine.

Weinlese: Harvest of grapes for wine making in the autumn.

Weinort: A village, the occupants of which are mainly *Weingärtner* or otherwise connected with the production of wine.

Westen: West.

Wetter: Weather.

Wetterfahne: Flag blowing in the wind, indicating the direction of the wind.

Wiedersehen: To see again. One says *"auf Wiedersehen"* upon departure.

Wirtschafts-Gymnasium: *Gymnasium* with emphasis on business subjects.

Wurst: Sausage. There are many kinds constituted of various meats and different parts of animals.

Zeile: Line.

zufrieden: Satisfied, content.

Zugezogener: Newcomer. In the context used in this book the term refers to *Flüchtlinge, Vertriebene*, and migrants into the Remstal from elsewhere in West Germany. It is a better term than "newcomer" for our purposes, since many *Zugezogenen* have been residents of the Remstal for more than twenty years.

References cited

Anderson, Nels, 1953, "A Community Study of Darmstadt, Germany," London: *Transactions of the Second World Congress of Sociology.*

Anderson, Robert, and Barbara Gallatin Anderson, 1965, *Bus Stop for Paris: The Transformation of a French Village.* New York: Doubleday & Company, Inc. (Anchor Books edition, 1966).

Anderson, Robert, 1971, *Traditional Europe: A Study in Anthropology and History.* Belmont, Calif.: Wadsworth Publishing Co., Inc.

Arensberg, Conrad M., 1963, "The Old World Peoples: The Place of European Authors in World Ethnography," *Anthropological Quarterly*, 36:75–99.

Bateson, Gregory, 1953, "An Analysis of the Nazi Film *Hitlerjunge Quex*" in *The Study of Culture at a Distance*, ed. by M. Mead and R. Metraux. Chicago: University of Chicago Press, pp. 302–314.

Bausinger, Herman, 1961, *Volkskultur in der Technischen Welt.* Stuttgart: W. Kohlhammer Verlag.

Binder, Gerhart, 1962, "Das Kreisgebiet im Gang de Geschichte" in *Der Kreis Waiblingen*, ed. by Konrad Theiss and Hermann Baumhauer. Aalen: Verlag Heimat und Wirtschaft, pp. 56–91.

Boissevain, Jeremy F., 1969, *Hal-Farrug: A Village in Malta* (Case Study in Cultural Anthropology). New York: Holt, Rinehart and Winston, Inc.

Bürgermeister, 1965. *Burgbacher Heimatbuch*, published under the auspices of the Gemeindeverwaltung Burgbach. Waiblingen, Fr. Spath KG.

Dahrendorf, Ralf, 1967, *Society and Democracy in Germany.* New York: Doubleday & Company, Inc.

Dicks, H. V., Lt. Col., R.A.M.C., 1944, *The Psychological Foundations of the Wehrmacht*, Directorate of Army Psychiatry, Research Memo. War Officer, London.

———, 1950a, "Some Psychological Studies of the German Character" in *Psychological Factors of Peace and War*, ed. by T. H. Pear. London: Hutchinson and Co., pp. 195–218.

———, 1950b, "Personality Traits and National Socialist Ideology," *Human Relations*, 3:111–154.

Dunn, Stephen P. and Ethel Dunn, 1967, *The Peasants of Central Russia* (Case Study in Cultural Anthropology). New York: Holt, Rinehart and Winston, Inc.

Ehni, Jörg, 1967, *Das Bild der Heimat im Schullesebuch*, Volksleben, Vol. 16. Tübingen: Tübinger Vereinigung für Volkskunde.

Elon, Amos, 1967, *Journey Through a Haunted Land: The New Germany.* London: André Deutsch Limited.

Epaus, E. Estyn, 1956, "The Ecology of Peasant Life in Western Europe" in *Man's Role in Changing the Face of the Earth*, ed., by W. Thomas, Jr. Chicago: University of Chicago Press.

Ethnology: an international journal of cultural and social anthropology. Vol. XI, No. 1, 1972.

Fishman, Joshua A., and Erika Lueders-Salmon, 1971, "What Has the Sociology of Language To Say to the Teacher?" (On Teaching the Standard Variety to Speakers of Dialectal or Sociolectal Varieties) in *Functions of Language,* ed. by C. B. Cazden, V. John, D. Hymes. New York: New York Teachers College Press.

Friedl, Ernestine, 1962, *Vasilika: A Village in Modern Greece* (Case Study in Cultural Anthropology). New York: Holt, Rinehart and Winston, Inc.

———, 1964, "Lagging Emulation in Post-peasant Society," *American Anthropologist*, 66:564–586.

Halpern, Joel M., 1972, *A Serbian Village in Historical Perspective* (Case Study in Cultural Anthropology). New York: Holt, Rinehart and Winston, Inc.

Halpern, Joel M., 1967, *The Changing Village Community.* Englewood Cliffs, N.J.: Prentice-Hall, Inc.

"Haus in der Heimat," Lesebuch für das dritte Schujahr der Volksschulen in Baden-Württemberg, 1957, Karlsruhe: Gemeinschaftsverlag.

Hofer, Tamás, 1968, Anthropologists and Native Ethnographers in Central European Villages: Comparative Notes on the Professional Personality of Two Disciplines, *Current Anthropology*, 9 (No. 4):311–315.

Honigmann, John, 1963, "Bauer and Arbeiter in a Rural Austrian Community," *Southwestern Journal of Anthropology*, 19:40–53.

Horkheimer, Max (ed.), 1936, *Studien über Autorität und Familie*, Paris: Librairie Felix Alcan.

Jacobet, W., 1961, "Sheep-keeping and the Shepherd in Central Europe up to the Beginning of the 20th Century," *Current Anthropology*, 2:269–270.

Kutter, V. W., 1966, "Towards a New Definition of Folk," *The Kroeber Anthropological Society Papers*, No. 34:83–90.

Lowie, Robert H., 1945, *The German People.* New York: Farrar & Rinehart, Inc.

———, 1954, *Towards Understanding Germany.* Chicago: The University of Chicago Press.

Marquardt, Ernst, 1962, *Geschichte Württembergs*, Stuttgart: J. B. Metzlersche Verlagsbuchhandlung.

Messenger, John C., 1969, *Inis Beag: Isle of Ireland* (Case Study in Cultural Anthropology). New York: Holt, Rinehart and Winston, Inc.

Metraux, Rhoda, 1955, "Parents and Children: An Analysis of Contemporary Child-Care and Youth Guidance Literature" in *Childhood in Contemporary Cultures*, ed. by M. Mead and M. Wolfenstein. Chicago: University of Chicago Press, pp. 204–228. (Phoenix edition, 1963). See also M. Mead's "Portrait of the Family in German Juvenile Fiction," and "The Consequences of Wrong-doing: An Analysis of Story Competitions by German Children" in the same volume.

Müller, Ernst, 1956, *Struktur Wandel des Dorfes.* Darmstadt: Arbeitsgenossenschaft Deutscher Lehrerverbände.

Nurge, Ethel, (no date), *Blue Light in the Village.* Unpublished manuscript.

Pitt-Rivers, Julian A., 1961, *The People of the Sierra.* Chicago: University of Chicago Press (Phoenix edition).

Pollock, Kurt, M.D., 1962, *Das Ärztliche Hausbuch.* München: Bertelsman Lesering Verlag.

Rahn, Fritz, 1962, *Der Schwäbische Mensch und Seine Mundart: Beiträge zum Schwäbischen Problem.* Stuttgart: Hans E. Gunther.

Roff, Adolf, 1958, *Unser Hausfreund*, Lorch: Karl Rohm Verlag.

Schaffner, Bertram, 1948, *Father Land.* New York: Columbia University Press.

Schmidberger, Fritz, 1956, *Gesundheit und Kräuter Bücher.* München: Alpenländisches Kräuterhaus.

Schmidt-Ebhausen, Friederich Heinz, 1965, *Schwäbische Volkssagen vom Schwarzwald zum Allgäu—vom Taubergrund zum Bodensee.* Stuttgart: W. Kohlhammer Verlag.

Schneiders, Rudolf, 1964, *Porträt des Dorfes: Gestern, Heute, Morgen.* München, Verlagsgesllschaft.

"Schwarz auf Weiss": Ein neues Lesebuch für Baden-Württemberg, Drittes Schuljahr, 1967, Darmstadt-Hanover: Herman Schroedel Verlag KG.

Schwedt, Herbert, 1968, *Kulturstile Kleiner Gemeinden*. Vol. 21. Tübinger Vereinigung für Volkskunde.

Spencer, Robert F., 1965, "The German Paradox," *The Journal of the Minnesota Academy of Science*, 32:3, 160–182.

Spindler, G. Dearborn (George D.), 1947, *Americans, Germans, and the Military*. Unpublished M. A. thesis, University of Wisconsin, Department of Sociology and Anthropology.

————, 1948, "American Character as Revealed by the Military," *Psychiatry: Journal for the Operational Statement of Interpersonal Relations*, 11 (No. 3): 275–281.

Spindler, George D., 1973, "Schooling in Schönhausen: A Study of Cultural Transmission and Instrumental Adaptation in an Urbanizing German Villege," in *Education and Cultural Process: Toward an Anthropology of Education*, ed. by G. Spindler. New York: Holt, Rinehart and Winston, Inc.

Spindler, George, and Louise Spindler, 1965, "The Instrumental Activities Inventory: A Technique for the Study of the Psychology of Aculturation," *Southwestern Journal of Anthropology*, 21 (No. 1):1–23.

Treinen, Heiner, 1965, *Symbolische Ortsbezogenheit: Eine soziologische Untersuchung zum Heimatproblem*, Inaugural Dissertation Köln und Opladen: Westdeutscher Verlag. (Also published in the Kölner Zeitschrift für Soziologie und Sozialpsychologie, Heft 1/2, 1965).

Vogt, Evon, and Ray Hyman, 1959, *Water Witching, U.S.A.* Chicago: University of Chicago Press.

Volz, Peter, 1969, *Das Remstal: Beispel einer grossstadtnahen Kulturlandschaft*. Stuttgart: Geographischen Instituts der Universität Stuttgart.

Warren, Richard L., 1967, *Education in Rebhausen: A German Village* (Case Study in Education and Culture). New York: Holt, Rinehart and Winston. Inc.

Weller, Karl, 1963, *Württembergische Geschichte*. Stuttgart: Selberburg Verlag.

Willems, Emilio, 1970, "Peasantry and City: Cultural Persistence and Change in Historical Perspective, A European Case," *American Anthropologist*, 72 (No. 3):528–544.

Wolfe, Eric R., 1962, "Cultural Dissonance in the Italian Alps," *Comparative Studies in Society and History*, 5 (No. 1): 1–14.

————, 1966, *Peasants*. Englewood Cliffs, N.J.: Prentice-Hall, Inc.

Wurzbacher, G., 1961, *Das Dorf im Spannungsfeld Industrieller Entwicklung*. Stuttgart: Ferdinand Enke Verlag.

Wylie, Laurence, 1957, *Village in the Vaucluse: An Account of Life in a French Village*. New York: Harper & Row, Publishers (Harper Colophon edition, 1964).

Recommended reading

Rather than the annotated bibliography which customarily ends case studies in this series we are supplying a brief review of existing materials relevant to this book, since there is actually little published on German villages, urbanizing or otherwise.

During and after World War II there was a spate of literature on German national character, the authoritarian personality of Germans, authoritarianism in German institutions, and the authoritarian tendencies in German families. In retrospect much of this literature seems biased as a result of the events of the times and the horror with which most of us viewed Nazism. Nevertheless, some of these publications are definitely worth reading if one wants to grasp some essential features of the larger picture. Even after the projection of bias stemming from the times is subtracted, there is something left that suggests that there are deep paradoxes in German culture and character. Of course, one must also make allowances for regional variation. The Remstal and Baden-Württemberg are not typical of the northern or even central parts of Germany. Part of the confrontation between newcomers and natives in the Remstal is the result of differences in degrees and kinds of authoritarianism, related in turn to differences in class structure. One can understand the differences better with a little background reading.

The papers by H. V. Dicks, an English psychiatrist who studied an extensive sample of German prisoners of war, are among the most adequate representations of an essentially psychological or psychiatric point of view incorporating the authoritarian hypothesis. He sees the basic personality trends as centering on compulsivity, stress on duty and submissive-dominant conformity (Dicks 1944, 1950a, 1950b). From the same period Bertram Schaffner, another psychiatrist, examines familial roles which he regards as the key to authoritarianism in the German character (Schaffner 1948). He is German-born and was Chief Psychiatrist for the Screening Center of the Information Control Division, established by the American Military Government to select Germans to work in the media.

Taking a different tack and with a different disciplinary background, Rhoda Metraux examines child-guidance books published in Germany between World War I and II. She finds that there are several consistent themes, such as obedience as a step to mastery, the dangers of spoiling and overprotection, the values of orderliness, and so forth, in this literature (Metraux 1963). A form of content analysis using another media is represented by the work of Gregory Bateson, "An Analysis of the Nazi Film *Hitlerjung Quex*" (Bateson 1953). A thoughtful review of long-term trends is provided by Robert Spencer, an anthropologist using a cultural framework in his analysis. He explains many of the traits explained by psychologists and psychiatrists in terms of family constellations by attention to the historical experience and geographical setting of Germany (Spencer 1965). Robert Lowie (1945 and 1954), the famous anthropologist whose best known work was with the Crow Indians, provides a fairly comprehensive cultural and social psychological analysis of German society and character, stressing the class structure and the absence of certain traditions present elsewhere in Europe as explanations of observed traits. For a recent evaluation of the more or less contemporary situation in Germany relevant to the social psychology of German society one should read Amos Elon's *Journey through a Haunted Land* (1967). There are many more works of the several kinds mentioned above. We have selected a few that we regard as most representative of important strategies of analysis. Anthropologists have been interested in Europe for some time and have written various things that are useful as background for case studies of particular communities, even though they are about more general matters. Epaus (1956) has analyzed the ecology of peasant life in western Europe. Kutter (1966) has compared definitions of "folk" by European ethnographers with anthropological concepts of folk used by non-Europeans. Willems (1970) has demonstrated how certain features of village and peasant life persisted in the village of Neyl as it became a part of the city of Cologne; how, in fact, industrial wage-earning was a means of preserving the essentials of a peasant way of life; and how folk and urban lifeways are not as opposed as the classic literature in anthropology would lead us to believe. Hofer (1968) has described the divergent strategies of European ethnographers, studying the peasantry and folklore in their own countries, and anthropologists, whose key approach has been the study of someone else's culture. The difficulties in communication are considerable. If Hofer's analysis is correct, our case study, in fact, may be criticized by European ethnographers as insufficiently related to the great mass of ethnography about the folk culture of the Remstal and Baden-Württemberg. This folk ethnography is highly interesting, but much of it is irrelevant to what we have been trying to develop as major themes in this book. Arensberg (1963) has argued for the treatment of Europe as a culture area, or areas, to be fit into a world-wide scheme of culture areas in a more-or-less traditional ethnological framework. This approach provides useful, but very general, background for studies of European villages. Robert Anderson (1971) has published a most useful cultural analysis of what he terms the "Traditional Europe" of the tenth through the eighteenth century, using anthropological concepts.

There have been some publications that have reviewed and integrated work done on peasant folk cultures and small communities that are very useful as background for this case study. Wolfe (1966) and Halpern (1967) are available in the Foundation of Modern Anthropology series. Halpern's is the most relevant for our purposes because he deals with urbanization in several national contexts, including socialist countries.

A number of studies have dealt with specific aspects of European communities. Honigmann (1963) studied a village in the Austrian Steiermark for two summers and has written about relationships between farmers and industrial workers. Friedl (1964) has written on a phenomenon she calls "lagging emulation" in the relationships between the rural and urban sectors of a national culture, in this case, mainland Greece. Wolfe (1962) has compared a German and an Italian village in the alpine Tyrol. He shows that despite very similar ecology, the social structure in the two villages is quite different. Jacobet (1961) has described sheep-keeping and the shepherd in central Europe. Patterns described by him can be seen in operation in the highlands near Burgbach. A recent issue of *Ethnology* (1972) includes papers on regional versions of Norwegian culture (Park), farm household and farm performance in southwest Ireland (Symes), bilingualism in southern Austria (Brudner), the social organization of Moslem slavs in western Bosnia (Lockwood), and tourism as an agent of change in a Spanish Basque village (Greenwood). There are many other such articles, but again, these selected few will give some indication of the type of materials available to the student. There appears to be a definite acceleration of publication and interest in the ethnography and social anthropology of Europe.

The literature in German is rich, but not in studies of single communities. There are two major types of studies in the published literature that are generally relevant to our concerns. One is the survey, more sociological-economic than anthropological in methods and concerns, such as Wurzbacher's (1961) study of villages under the influence of industrial development, or Müller's (1956) study of recent structural changes in villages, or Schneiders' (1964) generalized portrayal of the village in Germany over time—"yesterday, today, and tomorrow." The other is the literature produced by folklorists. There is a vast amount of this, most of it of high quality, amounting to a kind of national treasury of information about long-lapsed, or about to lapse, customs. Its relevance to the problems of studying the adaptation of the single small community to the impact of urbanization and industrialization is less than one might think, though some recent work in folklore (Volkskunde) is concerned with contemporary adaptations. It is useful to know something of the folk culture in its traditional forms, however, within an area if one is to consider the single community. The book by Rahn (1962) on the Swabians and their speech is one of the useful general pieces on the area and speech community of which the Remstal is a part. Schmidt-Ebhausen and Heinz (1965) furnish us with a fascinating popularized collection of schwäbisch folktales in the context of forest and mountain, house and barnyard in the Black Forest and elsewhere. The Tübinger Vereinigung für Volkskunde publishes excellent volumes of folkloristic research under the direction of Hermann Bausinger and his associates and much of this work has the orientation of cultural anthropology. Bausinger deviates considerably from what Americans think of as folkloristic research, methodology, and theory. His book on folk culture in the technical world (1961) is a very innovative analysis of the ways in which folk attitudes, such as personification of inanimate forces, and magical rituals, survive in the industrial environment. The German society for the study of folklore (Die Deutsche Gesellschaft für Volkskunde) has become heavily involved with problems of culture change, migration, acculturation, and urbanization. Little of the work so far produced is known to American anthropologists. Yet another approach is represented by a volume unknown to us until the spring of 1972 when the final revisions of this case study were being made: *Das Remstal: Beispiel einer grosstadtnahen Kulturlandschaft* by Peter Volz (1969).

Volz's work is within the emerging field of regional studies in the United States, and in Germany stems from the economic and social geographers. He has produced a most interesting analysis of interdependent ecological, demographic, economic, and historical factors in the Remstal, of which Burgbach and Schönhausen are a small part. Those who can read German and who are interested in a sophisticated and surprisingly complete analysis of this very interesting region would be well advised to read Volz's book. Our case study is quite different in its emphasis, not only because it is largely about one small community but because it is mainly involved with cultural processes.

There are a fair number of studies of small communities in European lands, though not as many as we would expect, given a long tradition of social sciences in Europe and strong American interest in things European. Some of the particularly notable ones are *Village in the Vaucluse*, a village in southern France, by Laurence Wylie (1957); Robert and Barbara Anderson's *Bus Stop for Paris* (1965), the transformation of a French village into a part of metropolitan Paris; Pitt-Rivers' *The People of the Sierra* (1961), a social structural analysis of a village, really a small town, in the mountains of Andalusia, in southern Spain. In the series, Case Studies in Cultural Anthropology, we have Jeremy Boissevain's *Hal-Farrug: A Village in Malta* (1969); John Messenger's *Inis Beag, Isle of Ireland* (1969), Ernestine Friedl's *Vasilika: A Village in Modern Greece* (1962); and Joel Halpern's *A Serbian Village in Historical Perspective* (1972). The Dunns' case study (1969) of the peasants of central Russia is useful for comparison to the situation behind the "iron curtain," for little is available in English as yet.

There are very few studies of villages or small communities in Germany, in either German or English. Nels Anderson has reported in English on an elaborate study of Darmstadt and its environs, carried out with American funds and by the Academy of Labor of the University of Frankfurt in 1949–1952, but the ten monographs in German, including one of the rural community within the area of influence of the city, have neither been translated into, or summarized, in English (Anderson 1953). To my knowledge there are no published studies of single villages in the anthropological tradition in Germany, by Germans, or by anyone else. However, as stated previously, there are great quantities of publication in folklore, folk sayings, proverbs, dialects, and a number of generalizing and survey-type studies. Herbert Schwedt (1968) has published a novel approach to the abstraction and description of the cultural styles of small German communities and their specific social and institutional correlates concentrating on one small town for illustration of interpretive generalizations. An excellent study of Burkhards, a village in central Germany, by Ethel Nurge, *Blue Light in the Village*, has not as yet been published. I have found Nurge's work to be very useful as comparative material. Richard Warren has written a study of education in Rebhausen, a village near Freiburg (Warren 1967), that should be read along with the present case study.

Student collaborators

The following students were in residence at Stanford in Germany during the times G. Spindler was teaching there. Though some contributed more directly than others to the accumulation of data and understandings upon which this case study is based, all are listed, for in one way or another, all helped.

Group III
Ahrens, Mia
Auster, Serena
Bailey, Anne
Barth, John
Beales, Ross
Bengson, Muriel
Bischoff, William
Brandt, Janice
Broemster, Gary
Brothers, Hannah
Casentini, Ronald
Cathcart, David
Chrisman, Keith
Clumeck, Jack
Corfino, George
Cunningham, Connie
Cutler, Sherilyn
Dallas, Allen
Ehlers, David
Faissler, Cynthia
Fellows, Carol
Fischer, David
Geisler, Gloria
Giarratana, Joseph
Gilchrist, Andrew
Gitielson, Bruce
Godfrey, Shirley
Goulter, Suzanne
Hahne, Marjorie
Hersh, Howard
Jacob, Esther
Jensen, Lin
Kent, Ann
Kettenring, Jon
Kienzie, Don
Koessler, Susan
Koff, David
La Breaux, Lynne
Lardner, Barbara
Markham, James
Marsh, Carol
Mendelson, Joan
Moser, Sally

Mullen, Margaret
Munger, Michael
Neeley, George
Nelson, Harvey
Page, Benjamin
Petrie, Brenda
Ringnalda, Karen
Sarkisian, Philip
Schou, Norman
Seinfeld, Dennis
Smilo, Susan
Speck, Stanley
Thias, Constance
Turbow, Myron
Verd, George
Vine, Don
Waswo, Richard
Whitney, Andree
Winbigler, Gail
Young, Norma

Group IV
Anderson, Stephen
Artman, Lynn
Bartizal, Henrietta
Baxter, Robert
Beattie, Karen
Behrman, Suzan
Bennett, John
Berkey, Edgar
Betts, Russell
Bradley, John
Breeden, Clara
Brown, Susan
Campbell, Mary
Chalmers, John
Cilley, Ann
Collins, Martha
Condit, Reid
Cook, Dale
Dean, Elizabeth
Deem, Gary
Dewell, Jacqueline
Elkind, Nina

Erdman, Mary
Fiske, Dixon
Fox, Herbert
Friedman, Ellen
Friel, Janette
Green, George
Gregory, Richard
Harden, Robert
Hillman, Elizabeth
Hopkins, Gregg
Hopkins, Richard
Hughes, Christopher
Hutton, Laurel
Jurras, Juliana
Kalin, Jesse
Keller, Ronald
Kirkish, Noel
Kline, Patricia
Lawry, James
Lenz, Andrew
Leonardson, Gene
Lowder, Judy
Maurer, Nancy
Mercer, George
Miller, Helen
Mitchell, Bridger
Moore, Walter
More, Katherine
Oakman, Wendy
Perry, Mark
Pierce, Daniel
Raynor, Judy
Reifler, Victoria
Robins, Shirley
Russell, Bonnie
Sable, Joseph
Singer, Carol
Sjoberg, Mildred
Smith, James
Train, Bruce
Tune, Bruce
Weedin, Everett
Weisgerber, Anne
Wilder, Gerissa

Wright, Ruhamah
Wyss, Trudy
Yap, Lorene

Group XVIII
Ashley, Margaret
Bauman, Jeffrey
Beckley, Terry
Beaver, Robert
Bell, Walter
Bruns, Loren
Buhl, Cheryl
Carrato, Joseph
Carter, Gretchen
Caves, Preston
Chapin, Douglas
Chase, Carol
Cummings, Steven
Curtiss, Steven
Egelko, Robert
Ekroth, Shirleen
Evans, David
Fisher, Judith
Fingado, Marta
Flower, Richard
Foote, Dennis
Fourr, Robert
Galton, Sidney
Granieri, Charles
Greene, Cherie
Hillis, Mark
Hiyane, Lani
Howard, Christy
Howe, Donna
Koda, Carole
Kokemoore, Richard
Lang, Pamela
Larrabee, James
Lee, Richard
Levin, Barbara
Lillis, Kathleen
Linkletter, Terence
Livingston, Stephen
Lutgert, Scott
McBirney, Kathy
Makela, Maria
Marks, Mary
Massey, James
Mendell, Laura
Meyer, William
Miller, Mary
Milton, Janet
Misczynski, Dean
Moseley, Fred
Munro, Allen
Neal, Howard
Nonnenberg, Alan
O'Brien, John
Olsen, Larry
Owen, Victor
Pepper, Stephen

Raynor, Douglas
Schwerdt, Elizabeth
Smith, Lura
Spector, Margaret
Speidel, Paul
Stewart, Paul
Templeton, Lynn
Textor, Stephen
Voss, Carl
Wattles, Janet
Wellman, Stewart
Wells, Jane
White, Eleanor
Wight, Edward
Yeilding, Nancy
Yelderman, Mark
Zalisk, Richard

Group XX
Albright, Samuel
Alden, David
Blumhagen, Joel
Bryson, Susan
Carstensen, Hans
Christopherson, Steven
Coleman, James
Crouse, Vonda
Cutten, Charles
Dankers, Hans
Davis, Scott
Denenholz, Cynthia
Denham, Janet
Denniston, Philip
Dilworth, Marilyn
Dougherty, Margaret
Eckhouse, John
Fahnestock, Mary
Gray, Barbara
Gray, Larry
Gruenbaum, Ellen
Guffey, Jerry
Hanson, Fredrick
Hearne, Stephanie
Hennings, Barry
Hill, Leslie
Hobbs, William
Howland, Edith
Hsu, Charlene
Jacobs, Stephen
Lambert, Thomas
Lightfoot, Dan
Linke, Harold
Luehring, Shirley
McLain, Gale
Maes, Gary
Magnuson, Michael
Mallory, Susan
Mayhew, Ellen
Miller, Craig
Miller, Robert
Moriarity, Penny

Moy, Thann
Murray, Christopher
Nagata, Anne
Page, Stephen
Pearson, Steven
Petrick, Gayle
Pfister, Thomas
Price, Bradley
Pyper, Joanna
Remund, Rene
Ryerson, Carlos
Ritter, Mary
Sandberg, David
Scott, Martha
Shaw, William
Shelton, Robert
Southard, Douglas
Spickard, James
Stein, Morton
Stiles, Robert
Stanislaw, Marie
Stone, Barbara
Tanaka, Karen
Tubman, Richard
Van DeVanter, Michael
Vernon, Brent
Viken, Richard
Wee, Morris
White, Geoffrey
Wiley, Charles
Willard, Patricia
Williams, Scott
Wineberg, Ellin
Woolley, John
Wright, Diane
Wright, Marcy
Wyss, John
Young, Kay
Zanides, Mark

Group XXIV
Ambler, Samuel
Barber, Emma
Barnard, Mark
Beck, Bruce
Bingham, Gail
Bjorklund, Pamela
Blasberg, Steven
Brennan, Anne
Brunsman, John
Bush, Lloyd
Chinn, Carol-Jo
Comann, Tylor
Crandell, Ashley
Dahl, Patricia
Darby, Ann
Deeringer, James
Denenholz, Deborah
Ditchey, Roy
Donnen, James
Egg, Alan

Feuerstein, James
Funamaura, Jack
Gibson, Linda
Guntermann, Penelope
Haley, Carol
Hannah, Richard
Hazlett, Mark
Heffern, Edward
Hefsen, David
Helsell, Katherine
Heuscher, Enno
Hickam, David
Hiseler, Beth
Howard, John
Jensen, Peter
Kasbeer, Richard
Kauhanen, Keith
Koester, Crystell
Lang, James
Lavalley, William
Lawry, George
Leidersdorf, Craig
Liner, Marilyn
Loy, Janwyn
McCoy, Thomas
McGuinness, Shawn
Malinowski, Melvin
Merrell, Thomas
Miller, Nicholas
More, Sara
Moore, Walter
Mowery, Carol
Newmark, Lucy
Olsen, Philip
Olson, Patricia
Olson, Robert
Payne, Judith
Pedersen, Maren
Pullen, Jennifer
Ramsey, Robert
Redburn, Chris
Reichert, William
Schroeckenstein, David
Scott, James
Shelton, Earl
Skomer, Charles
Steinle, Kathleen
Thorpe, Allan
Thulin, Charles
Tolan, Tod

Tollerud, David
Stone, Karen
Tomlinson, Carol
Towner, Robert
Trompas, Emily
Vierling, David
Wallace, Robert
Whitehouse, Lauren
Williams, Kristen
Yaholkovsky, Peter

Group XXVI
Adams, Lynda
Alden, Merritt
Allen, Deborah
Araki, Warren
Atkinson, Steven
Barnes, Randall
Bennett, Charles
Bold, Jane
Burgess, Mary
Camm, Arlene
Camp, Donald
Capri, Mark
Carson, David
Cheronis, John
Chew, Stephanie
Clark, Carolyn
Cole, Daniel
Combs, Stephen
Creighton, Karyn
Cumming, Donald
Daugherty, Robert
Decker, Pamela
Dehnert, James
De Prez, Gregory
Drennan, Michael
Duffy, Michael
Durbin, Anna
Dyer, Carolyn
Dyer, Charles
Edmunds, Wesley
Ehrlichman, Peter
Fenno, Marion
Field, Carl
Fletcher, Michael
Flohr, Thomas
Gonzalez, Carol
Grether, John
Heninger, Kathryn

Hinton, Bruce
Hollenbach, Janet
Hook, Robert
Hornbeak, Tom
Hunt, Stephen
Ikeda, Dale
Johnson, Mark
Kraft, Kenneth
Kratka, Guynoir
Larson, Lois
Larson, Robert
Lima, David
Linvill, Candace
Lowe, Janice
Lyddon, Margaret
MacGregor, William
McGeary, Scott
Milburn, Michael
Mittelstaedt, Brian
Monteverde, Kirk
Muller, Susan
Nemec, Neil
Neville, Mary
Oleson, Raymond
Oliver, John
Oswald, Susan
Pete, Robert
Peterson, Kathleen
Phillips, John
Prudek, Fred
Redenbaugh, John
Rombach, Brigitte
Rooke, George
Satre, Philip
Schoknecht, Kurt
Scurlock, Donna
Shackelford, Charles
Shaffer, Evan
Shawcroft, Robert
Smith, David
Springer, Jennifer
Stoebner, Kerry
Stolte, Cynda
Talbot, Susan
Von Stade, Philip
Wainwright, Carol
Washburn, John
Wong, David
Wright, Victoria
Wyss, Claudia

DATE DUE

FEB 12 '87			
GAYLORD			PRINTED IN U.S.A.